GRIEG

Thirty-eight Pianoforte Pieces

Book I

Selected and edited by

ANGUS MORRISON

THE ASSOCIATED BOARD OF
THE ROYAL SCHOOLS OF MUSIC

£5.75

THEMATIC INDEX

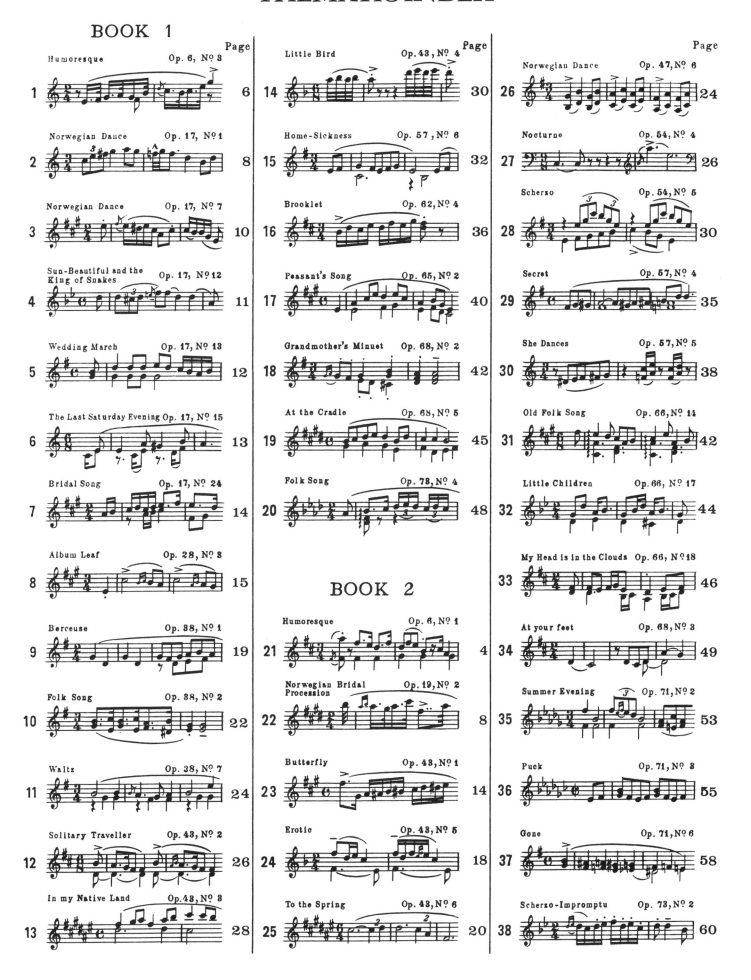

FOREWORD

In making this selection of Grieg's pianoforte pieces I have tried throughout to maintain an even balance between the familiar and the unfamiliar. From one point of view it would be tempting to omit all the popular favourites and concentrate on lesser-known pieces only, but it must be remembered that some of the hackneyed pieces are the most perfect, and it is only because they have so often been played badly and sentimentally that this tends to be forgotten. No apology therefore is offered for including such pieces as 'Berceuse', 'Butterfly', 'To the Spring', etc; they are among the loveliest works Grieg ever wrote, and indispensable to a true appreciation of his art and inspiration. In addition to the ten books of Lyric Pieces and other sets of original pieces I have also drawn on the two groups of folksong arrangements, Op.17 and Op.66. Some are perhaps a little perfunctory, but the best of them have the same charm and finish, the same right to be included in these volumes as other pieces in the Norwegian folk-idiom found amongst the Lyric Pieces and elsewhere.

With a composer of such exquisite craftsmanship as Grieg the task of an editor is an easy one, and I have added practically nothing in the way of phrasing and expression marks. His own markings in these respects are exemplary in their clarity, and always explicit in indicating the right style and mood for each piece.

The question of pedalling, however, is not so easy. Here his indications are less explicit, and it is more than probable that he himself used the pedal so instinctively that it was difficult for him to analyse and transcribe accurately such an almost unconscious process. In many places I have added supplementary pedal marks – always in brackets – but in certain slow, sustained pieces of a lyrical character, such as 'In my Native Land' and 'At the Cradle' (Book I) and 'Erotic', 'Secret' and 'At your Feet' (Book II) it would be impossible to indicate the many infinitely subtle changes and half-changes required. Here the ear of the player must be the final guide in creating the right effect; one of great warmth and richness of tone combined with the utmost clarity of line and progression.

Then there are the ornaments. Grieg uses either a single note, written invariably as an *acciaccatura,* or an upward turn, written sometimes as two small semiquavers, sometimes with the sign ⌒ and occasionally as two ordinary demisemiquavers forming an integral part of the phrase. Personally I think these differences of notation are largely fortuitous, and that, except possibly in a few places, Grieg intended all ornaments to be played firmly and clearly *on* the beat, in strict accordance with classical usage. This indeed is self-evident, (a) where they are written out, (b) where the classical sign ⌒ is used, and (c) where the small turn follows a semiquaver or demisemiquaver at the end of the previous beat, as in the middle section of 'Album Leaf' No.3 (Book I) or in 'Norwegian Bridal Procession' (Book II). The only places in which this rule might be relaxed are sustained melodies where the turn follows a long held note, and other passages where a predominantly expressive effect is required. The same applies to the *acciaccaturas.* In the majority of cases these are purely rhythmical and should be played *with* the bass note, but when they occur in an expressive melodic line it is permissible, and sometimes necessary, to play them just before the beat.

Finally, a word about repeats. In many pieces Grieg had repeated sections printed out in full, and there is no doubt that he considered this essential in order to give each piece its right proportions. For convenience some of these repeats have been condensed by the use of repeat signs, but all should be scrupulously observed in performance, in order to preserve the form and symmetry conceived by the composer.

ANGUS MORRISON

HUMORESQUE

GRIEG, Op. 6, N? 3

Allegretto con grazia

NORWEGIAN DANCE

GRIEG, Op. 17, Nº 1

NORWEGIAN DANCE

GRIEG, Op. 17, № 7

SUN - BEAUTIFUL AND THE KING OF SNAKES

GRIEG, Op. 17, No 12

WEDDING MARCH

GRIEG, Op. 17, № 13

THE LAST SATURDAY EVENING

GRIEG, Op. 17, № 15

BRIDAL SONG

GRIEG, Op. 17, Nº 24

ALBUM LEAF

GRIEG, Op. 28, No 3

BERCEUSE

GRIEG, Op. 38, N⁰ 1

FOLK SONG

GRIEG, Op. 38, N.º 2

WALTZ

GRIEG, Op. 38, № 7

Tempo I

ritard.

p a tempo

cresc.

ritardando

Lento

SOLITARY TRAVELLER

GRIEG, Op. 43, № 2

IN MY NATIVE LAND

GRIEG, Op. 43, Nº 8

LITTLE BIRD

GRIEG, Op. 43, No 4

Allegro leggiero

HOME – SICKNESS

GRIEG, Op. 57, N° 6

In the original edition the repeat of the second half of the middle section was printed in full. This repeat should of course be observed in performance.

In the twelfth bar of the middle section there is uncertainty about the fourth semi-quaver in the right hand — should it be ♮ or ♯? Misprints are very rare in Grieg's music, but here I have no doubt that by some oversight the accidental was printed next to the second B instead of the first. A. M.

A B 1379

BROOKLET

GRIEG, Op. 62, N.º 4

In the original edition both repeats were printed in full. These repeats should of course be observed in performance.

A B 1379

PEASANT'S SONG

GRIEG, Op. 65, Nº 2

GRANDMOTHER'S MINUET

GRIEG, Op. 68, No 2

In the original edition the repeat of the second half was printed in full. This repeat should of course be observed in performance.

AT THE CRADLE

GRIEG, Op. 68, No. 5

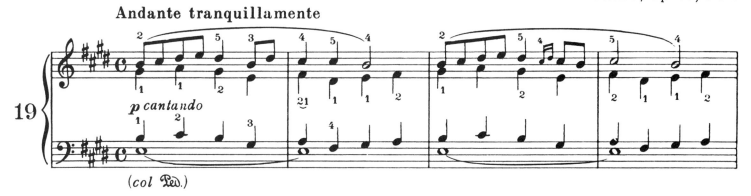

FOLK SONG

GRIEG, Op. 73, № 4

Printed in England by Caligraving Limited, Thetford, Norfolk   A B 1379   11:92

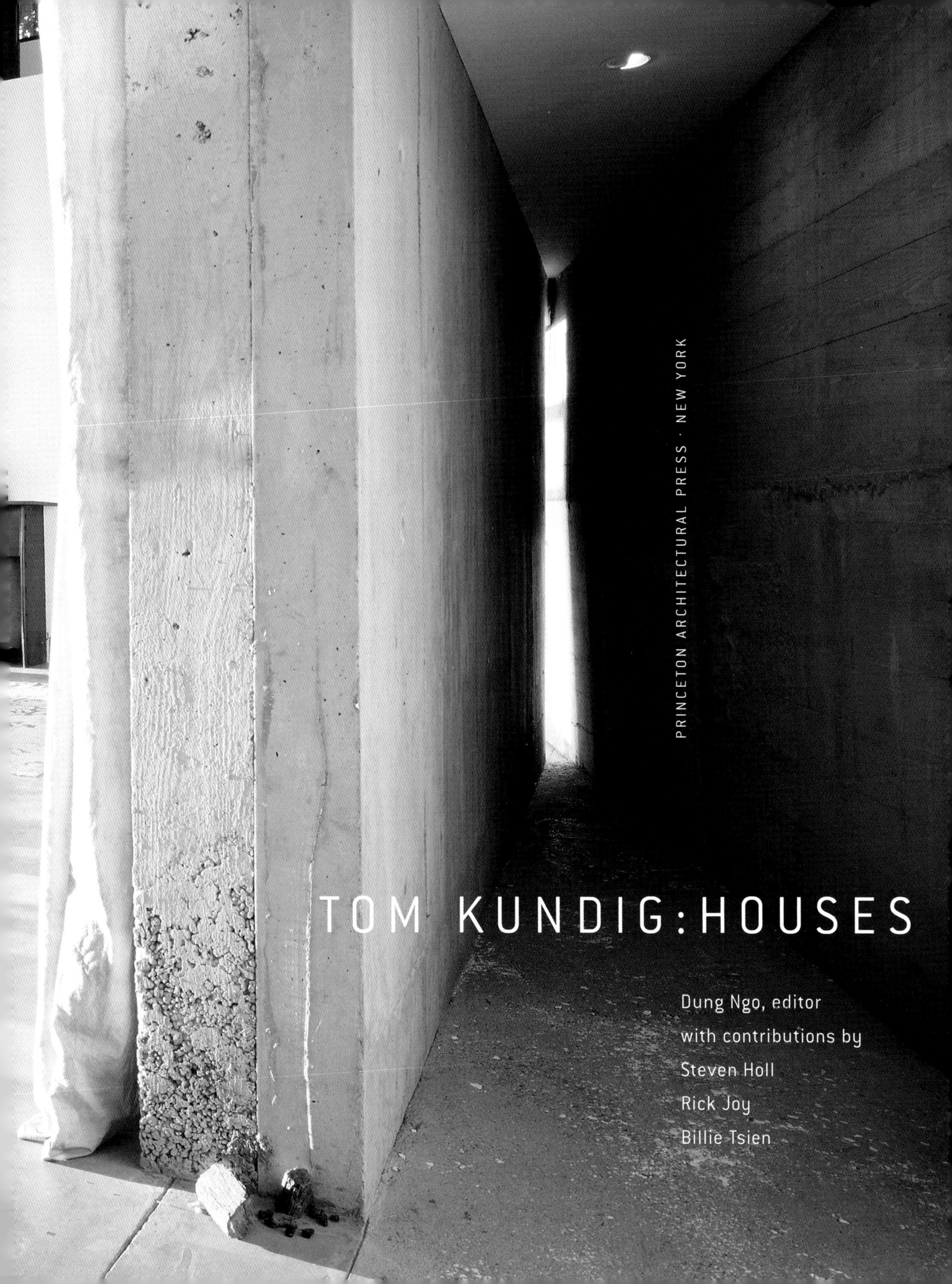

PRINCETON ARCHITECTURAL PRESS · NEW YORK

TOM KUNDIG:HOUSES

Dung Ngo, editor

with contributions by

Steven Holl

Rick Joy

Billie Tsien

PREFACE
TOM KUNDIG

In the original preface to *Tom Kundig: Houses*, I described this book—and, effectively, my career to date—as an eye blink. The opportunity to put a book together came at a pivotal moment, the perfect storm of maturity and experience, youth and curiosity. At that time, it seemed that all my various paths of inquiry were coming together into a coherent practice, ultimately creating a launching pad for an approach to design that continues today.

Though I have worked on many, many projects since, the five featured in this book are special. This book came at an important point in my career, when I truly began to find my voice as a designer; these five projects provided a foundation for subsequent pursuits and discoveries, a launching point for future journeys. I've been incredibly lucky to work with clients who are engaged during the process of design and who remain friends long after construction is finished. I've had the good fortune to revisit these houses over the years, to see how they've aged and improved over time, as all good architecture should. I still live in Hot Rod House with my wife, Jeannie. The house remains a valuable research laboratory, with ongoing R & D efforts and experiments that inevitably influence other projects. Living in the midst of those experiments has been incredibly valuable to my career, helping me to understand how my micro-level decisions impact the experience of the built work and how to improve that work.

I hope that this book, like a building, has gotten better with age. *Tom Kundig: Houses* is a tactile distillation of many different ideas and experiences, a physical record released into our increasingly digital, ephemeral world. Though I don't spend a lot of time in academic spheres, I have heard from architecture students through the years that this book impacted their education. It has provided a kind of extension course of independent study for the curious, perhaps started conversations that helped to sharpen their own point of view. As a platform to share what I have learned with the next generation of creative, innovative designers, this book is as much a part of my legacy as any building I've designed.

Back in 2006, Princeton Architectural Press took a chance on me by publishing this book. I could not have guessed then that more volumes would follow, and I remain deeply appreciative of and deeply humbled by their confidence. (As I write this, my fourth monograph with Princeton Architectural Press, *Tom Kundig: Working Title*, has just been released.) In the intervening years, my list of indebtedness has only continued to grow; the people, encounters, and experiences that have shaped my career remain impossible to tally. Instead, I return to the list first published in *Tom Kundig: Houses*, to once again thank the people who challenged and inspired and believed in me so many years ago:

My parents, Moritz and Dora, who had the courage to leave Switzerland in 1952 for the big sky, open landscape, and characters of the North American West.

John Jochman—a friend and fellow skeptical architect, whose early death cut short finding direction for his immense talent; Gerry Cichanski, for his support for living outside the culture of architecture; Gary Nicholas and Charlotte Oberst, for always being there; Dave and Diana Dailey, for countless high mountain epics and a friendship forged under Full Conditions.

Astra Zarina and Herman Pundt, professors with hearts of artists and poets; Steven Holl, professor and friend, an artist whose medium happens to be architecture; Rick Joy, a poet-of-place who is working at a higher plane than the rest of us mortals, and a friend; Billie Tsien, an immensely gifted architect who understands the heart of humanness and the soul of humanity.

Jim Olson, for supporting our divergent instincts as well as common interests and for his wisdom, which will lead the firm he founded into a long future beyond our wonderful mess; Kirsten Murray and Alan Maskin—in our familiar, stressful, wonderfully difficult profession, their support has not gone unnoticed: Kirsten, for her smart, bedrock-steady support through thick and thin, Alan, for his incredible sense of what is good, right, and wonderful; Kevin Kudo-King, who joined the Olson Kundig ownership group in 2015, for his relentless commitment to architecture and its boundless potential; Matt Anderson, for his madman juggling and frenetic hard work, balancing a marketing effort and multiple book projects and for shipping me off to the MacDowell Colony; Evan Harlan, for his tested patience and for producing the wonderful hard line drawings in the book; the staff of Olson Sundberg Kundig Allen Architects (now Olson Kundig). The architect working alone is a myth; the future of the firm exists because the staff is busily working, learning, and developing a distinct direction of our own that will carry us into an unknown but exciting future.

Clients, for their emotional and financial risk-taking in a poetic science (architecture is not a money-back-if-not-completely-satisfied deal); Carol Bobo, whom I cannot thank enough. She has an artist's heart of the highest order that sensed something in me and trusted an unknown to make architecture; David Wild and Lulu Gargiulo: What could be better than making a magical place with friends? Jeff and Amy Larson, who supported, trusted, and laughed with us while we danced; Michal Friedrich, for the absolute courage to live life at its fullest.

The craftsmen, engineers, and contractors who are willing to learn, teach, and take chances—all of whom are necessary in creating meaningful work; David Gulassa, for the magic that happens when art and craft are seamless; Phil Turner, for the pure delight of understanding and tinkering with the movement of our world.

The photographers—Benjamin Benschneider, Tim Bies, Mark Darley, Undine Prohl, Marco Prozzo, and Paul Warchol—you are all magicians and masochists who photograph architecture; Dung Ngo for searching me out and wanting the work to get out there, and for his incredibly charming, talented, and patient manner.

In the end, I'm left with two very special people whose presence is felt in every project:

Harold Balazs—sculptor, artist, mentor, force of nature. As a child, I was lucky to witness the artist's heart. I learned about the willingness to work relentlessly, take risks, avoid bureaucracies, laugh at the absurdity of life, and—most important—I learned that it's not about the art, it's about the world.

And finally, Jeannie, the love of my life, I could not have done it without you.

—Tom Kundig

The client, Carol Bobo, is a photographer and artist who bought the site from an old friend in order to build a house and studio. Situated on a bluff facing west to Puget Sound, the site is surrounded by mature Douglas fir and washed in natural light. To honor Carol's friend who had passed away, Tom Kundig decided to keep one of the walls of the old house and incorporate it into the new design. The remnant wall became an integral part of the shifted entry sequence, moving from the old to the new.

The heart of the house is a large rectangular volume with a gently vaulted roof, containing the kitchen, living area, and dining area, all of which can be rearranged and converted into a workspace or photography studio. The large west-facing glass wall flooding the space with natural light can also be covered up with curtains for studio photo shoots. Uplights and spotlights are hung off the steel structure, which is left unfinished, the material's natural aging process being part of the design intention.

With the encouragement of the client, many pieces of the interior were custom-made, including the fireplace, the kitchen island, and most of the hardware. This is also true for the cabinetry in the home office, the bedrooms, and the fixtures in the bathrooms, which are located in double-story volumes on either side of the main space.

The Studio House is a watershed project for Tom, where he established an architectural language of materials, construction methods, and details—all of which he refined and drew from for subsequent projects, especially the houses in this publication. Perhaps the most important breakthrough of the Studio House is a set of working methodologies that allowed for experimentation and collaboration with the clients, contractors, and craftsmen who contributed to the project's design and production.

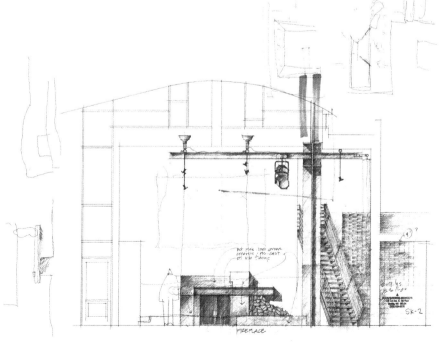

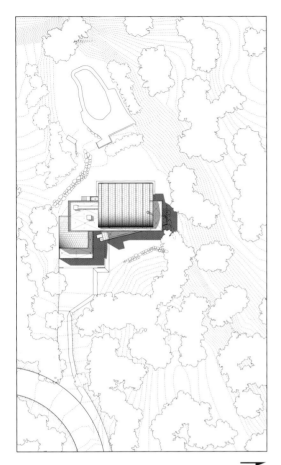

SITE PLAN

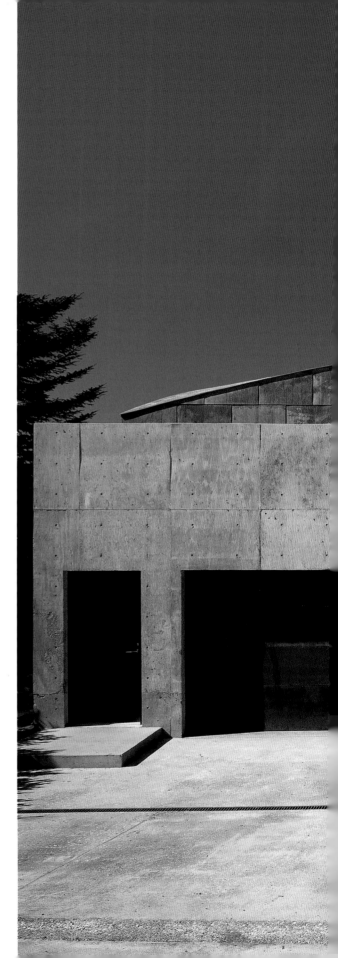

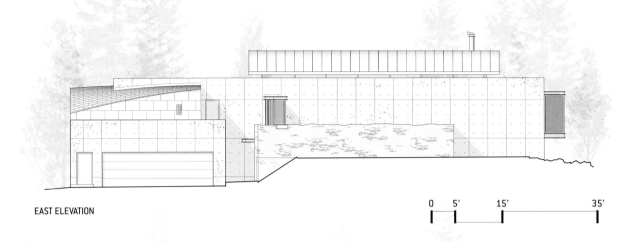

EAST ELEVATION

0   5'   15'   35'

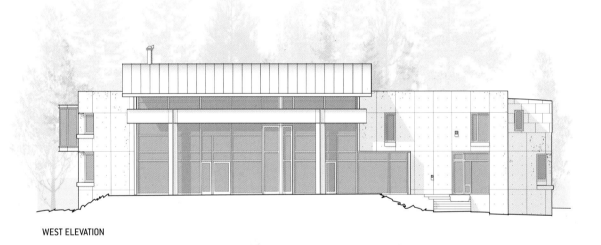

WEST ELEVATION

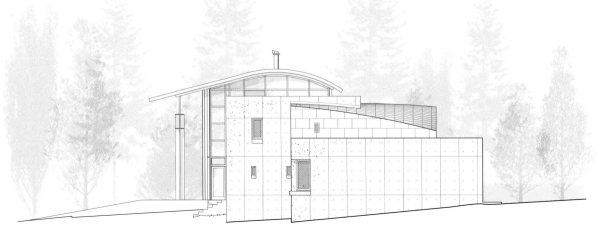

SOUTH ELEVATION

The remnant wall of the previous house on the site became the generative basis of the angled entry sequence, which is marked by a steel-and-glass "lantern," the only focal point on this otherwise opaque facade. The oversized front door modulates between the mature trees on the surrounding site and the relatively intimate foyer.

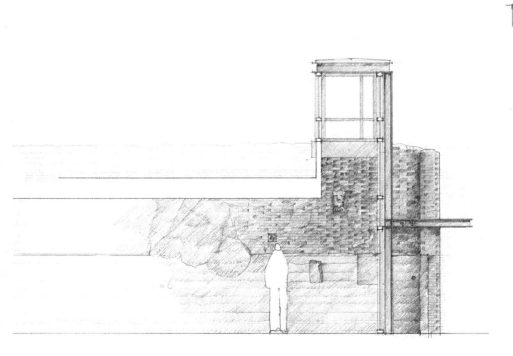

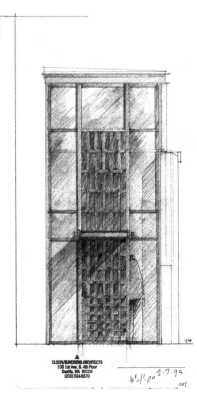

1 OFFICE
2 OPEN TO BELOW
3 GUEST SUITE
4 CARETAKER'S SUITE

SECOND FLOOR

1 STUDIO
2 SITTING AREA
3 WORK/DINING AREA
4 KITCHEN
5 ENTRY
6 PORCH
7 MASTER BEDROOM
8 MASTER BATH
9 CLOSET

GROUND FLOOR

0 5'   15'   35'

1 CLOSET
2 UTILITY ROOM
3 STORAGE

BASEMENT

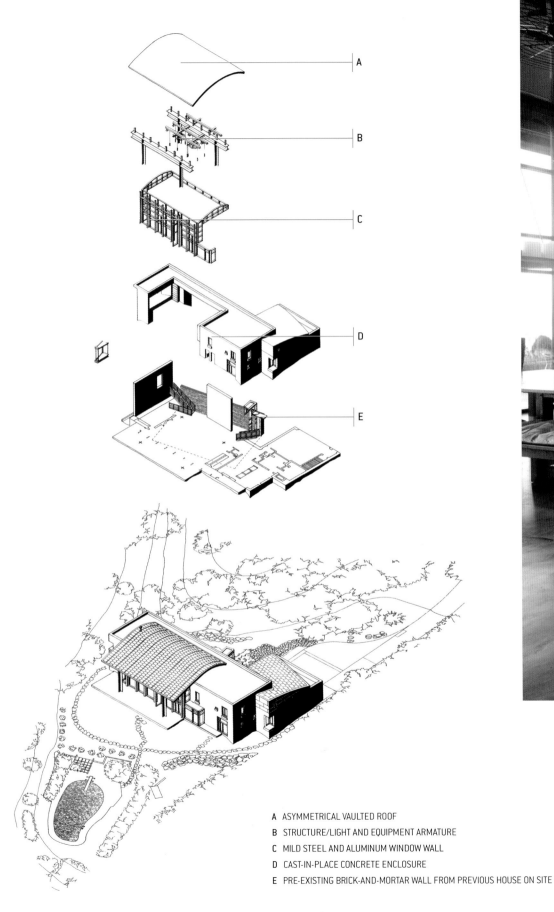

A ASYMMETRICAL VAULTED ROOF

B STRUCTURE/LIGHT AND EQUIPMENT ARMATURE

C MILD STEEL AND ALUMINUM WINDOW WALL

D CAST-IN-PLACE CONCRETE ENCLOSURE

E PRE-EXISTING BRICK-AND-MORTAR WALL FROM PREVIOUS HOUSE ON SITE

The steel framework of the main volume also doubles as an armature for a variety of uplights, spotlights, and a candle chandelier. Tom collaborated with Carol Bobo, the owner, and David Gulassa, a local metal worker, to produce various custom pieces. The uplights were made by David on an English Wheel machine, which produces semispherical shapes from flat steel sheets. The semispheres are then sliced and welded together to the final "beetle shell" forms.

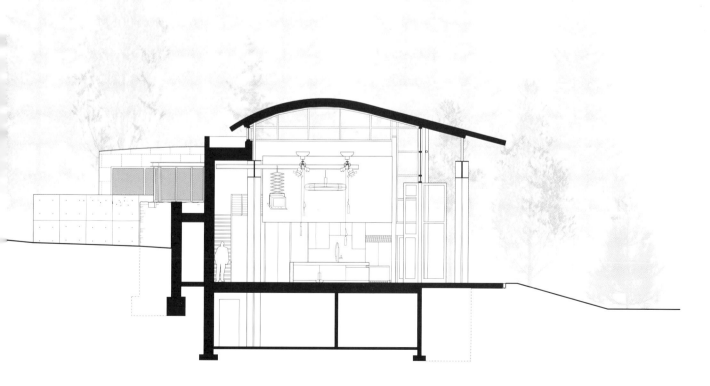

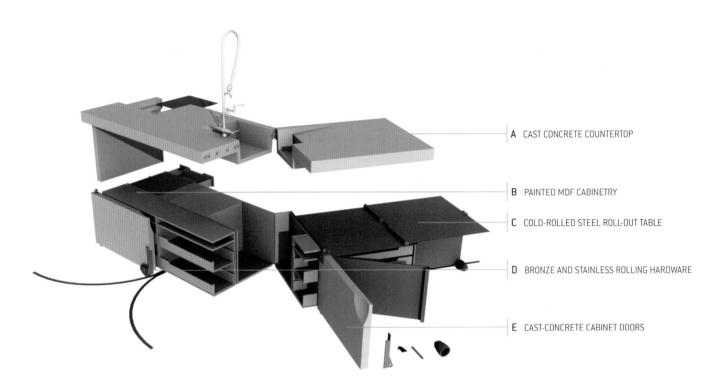

A   CAST CONCRETE COUNTERTOP

B   PAINTED MDF CABINETRY

C   COLD-ROLLED STEEL ROLL-OUT TABLE

D   BRONZE AND STAINLESS ROLLING HARDWARE

E   CAST-CONCRETE CABINET DOORS

The kitchen island is another collaboration between Tom and Gulassa Metalworks along with another subcontractor who produced the cast-concrete top and rolling doors. The larger metal surfaces and cast-in-floor rolling tracks are patinated steel, while the hardware and wheels are cast bronze.

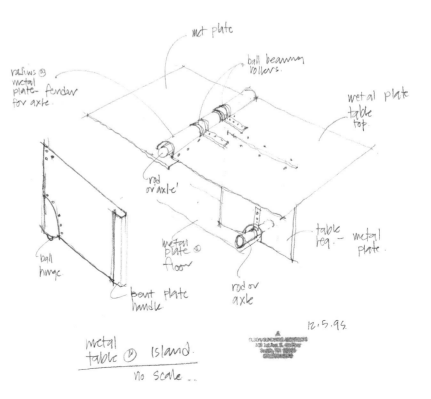

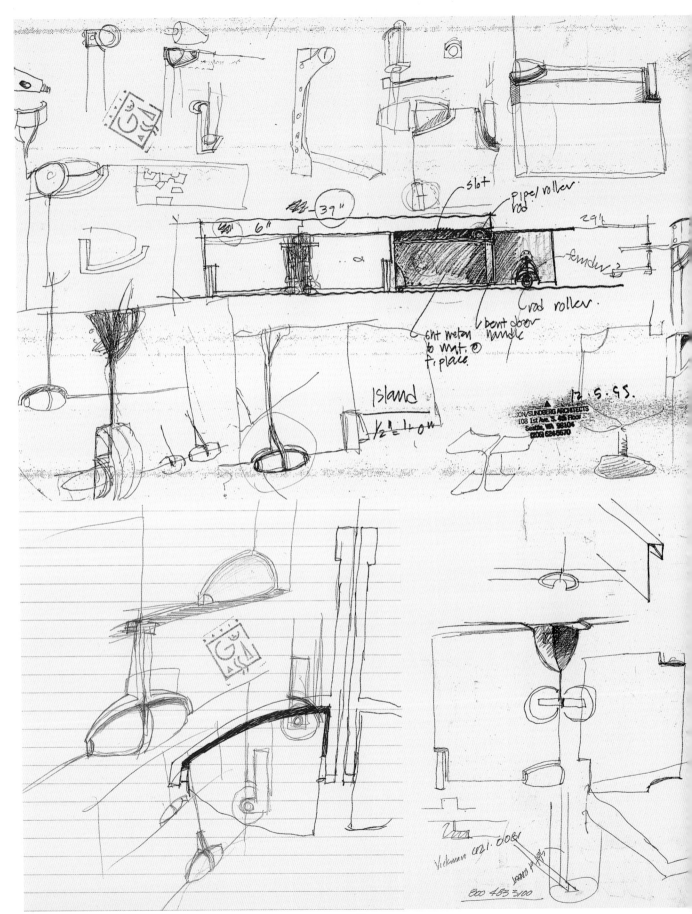

slot

Pipe/roller
rod/roller

6"

39"

29"

fender

rod roller

bent door
handle

cut metal
to mat. @
f. place.

Island
½"=1'-0"

12.5.95.

OLSON/SUNDBERG ARCHITECTS
108 1st Ave. S. 4th Floor
Seattle, WA 98104
(206) 624-5670

Vickman 0021.0061

800 483 3100

30

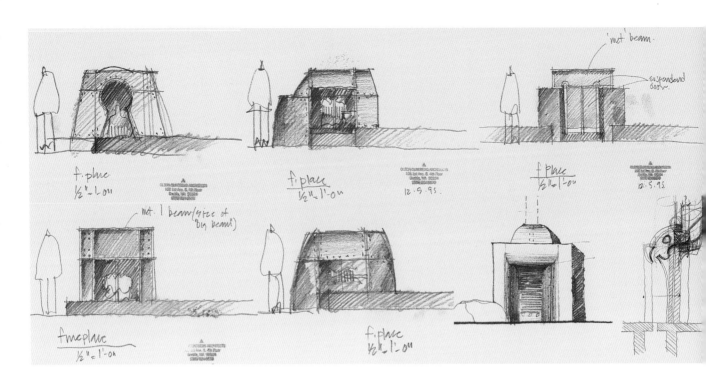

Various configurations of the gas fireplace placed opposite the kitchen island were sketched and mocked-up. The final design is constructed of blackened steel, the same material as the custom uplights.

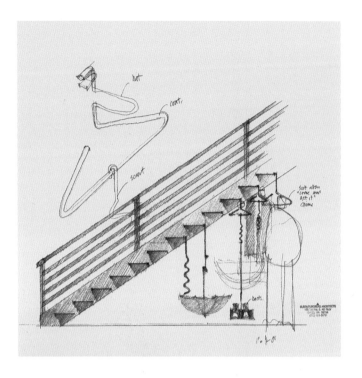

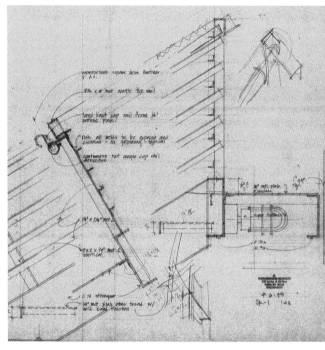

The steel staircases throughout the house mediate between the smaller, more refined elements such as the fireplace and the larger exposed steel structure and light armature. Although the stairs are less detailed and "finished" than the other pieces, they are just as carefully designed and considered. The stairs—along with the kitchen island, fireplace, powder room, and master bathroom—can be seen as pieces of micro-architecture: smaller tectonic versions of the larger house.

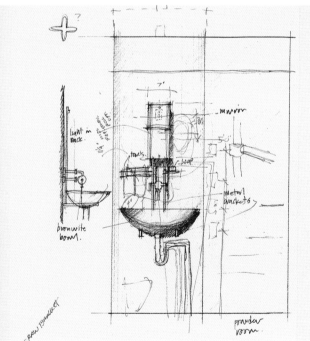

The guest powder room is a deliberate exercise in mock frustration, with "a mirror that's too small, a shallow sink that splashes water onto your pants, and no shelf for personal effects," according to Tom. Humor and wit turn a source of potential irritation into visual elegance.

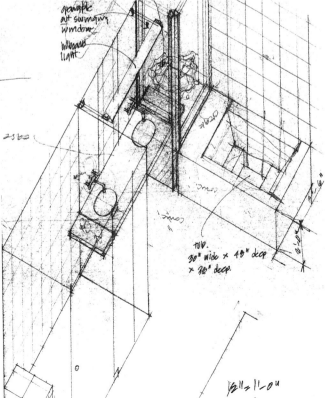

The master bathroom is as much a tactile and visual delight as the most public spaces in the house. Employing the same palette of cast concrete and exposed steel frame, it manages to exude relaxation and calm through the generous proportions and views to the verdant outdoors. The stainless steel medicine cabinet was designed by Janice Viekman, who acted as consulting interior designer on the project.

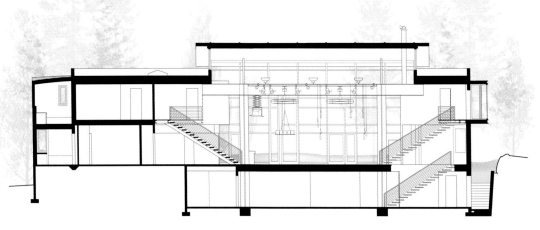

In Tom Kundig's office—at Olson Sundberg Kundig Allen Architects in Seattle, where Tom is a partner—there is one of his trademark mechanical devices in the central lightwell. The highly articulated contraption is operated by two simple mechanical disc levers accessed from the glass and steel bridge. With the slightest effort a three-ton steel and glass sky-door moves noiselessly open (figures 1, 2, 3). In our high-tech digital age of wireless devices, the act of effortlessly moving several tons of building material at the turn of a lever brings out the giddy kid in all of us. Childlike wonderment turns into incredulity, however, when it is learned that the force to open the contraption is powered solely by the pressure of Seattle's water supply system. Utilizing the forty pounds-per-square-inch pressure of the city's water—aided by a counter-balance ballast—an existing, untapped powersource is surreptitiously pressed into service, bringing fresh air and light into the two-story office space. As sunlight rakes across the steel frame overhead during the course of the day, a subtle play of shadows and light displays itself on the "blank canvas" of the white wall adjacent to the cross-bridge, creating an ever-changing light monitor and modulator (figure 4). As is often the case when encountering Tom's work, the first jolt of bravura is immediately followed by a host of mature concerns for his sophisticated use of materials and construction, clarity of proportion and space, a reverence for light and the natural landscape, along with the unexpected and a sly sense of humor that shows itself in ways large and small.

FOUNDATIONS

When Tom's work first began to appear in trade publications and newspapers in the early 1990s, there was not only a recognition of an emerging, undeniable talent, but also the shock that such mature work seemed to have came "out of nowhere." Seattle was never one of the more scrutinized centers of news before the technology boom, and even after Microsoft, Starbucks, and Amazon changed the way we live, scant attention has been paid to the art and design scene there. In fact, the Pacific Northwest has long been an incubator of a unique craft-based architecture and design culture that draws upon both its industrial and timber heritage. George Nakashima and Steven Holl are but two talents of the many in the past half century that have come out of this particular milieu. Though both settled and made their careers on the east coast, they brought with them the arts-and-crafts tradition instilled by their training from this corner of the country, the geographic and cultural region where Tom Kundig is a native.

Tom's parents emigrated from Switzerland to the United States after World War II. Moritz Kundig, Tom's father, is an architect who was trained at the ETH in Zurich (the famed Swiss Federal Institute of Technology) in the strictest tenets of European modernism. After coming to the United States, the Kundigs settled in Spokane, Washington, and became an integral part of its fledgling cultural community, a group of artists and designers who were spurred by the optimism of postwar zeitgeist to develop integrated and collaborative practices. The senior Kundig often worked with local artists and designers on civic and residential commissions; and a number of the libraries and churches designed collaboratively with fellow artists and craftsmen still stand today in the Spokane area. Harold Balazs, one of Moritz Kundig's most frequent artistic associates, is a sculptor Tom cites as one of the seminal influences on his thinking and design philosophy (figure 5). As a young man, Tom worked summers for Balazs as an assistant where he was drawn to the sculptor's tireless enthusiasm and freewheeling attitude toward the production of art. Balazs is one of those artists known to climb on top of a "finished" and installed piece of art to make "improvements." Working in Balazs's frenetic studio showed Tom that artistic production could be spontaneous and intuitive as well as delib-

FIG.1   FIG. 2   FIG. 3

erate and painstaking. Although Tom did not know at this early age that he would become an architect, his working experience and enduring friendship with Balazs allowed Tom to think of the architectural enterprise as expansive and inclusive instead of the introspective and contemplative endeavors encountered in school. More than anything, it was Balazs's unmediated engagement to materials, to production techniques, and to the place and people who would encounter his commissioned work on a daily basis that remained with Tom from these early days.

Tom claims to have been a restless student during architecture school. Though there were a number of inspired teachers at the University of Washington, including Steven Holl and Astra Zarina (who also taught Holl when he was in school there), Tom remembers those years and the first decade of his career as "the lost years," when he was finding his footing and passion not in architectural practice but in technical alpine mountain climbing. The sport allowed Tom to pursue his direct engagement with the natural landscape of the Northwest in ways that school could never offer. Although it was initially an escape from the stress of school and work, the skill and rigor of the sport found a place in his later work in ways that he could not have anticipated; climbing requires the heightening of all the senses, especially the sense of touch, materiality, and tactility; characteristics that became of utmost importance to Tom's architecture.

After working for several firms in the Northwest and in Switzerland (including having his own firm in Alaska), Tom joined the firm of Olson Sundberg Architects in Seattle. At that time, as it is now, it was considered one of a handful of top architecture firms in the Northwest producing exceptional work. In Jim Olson Tom found a colleague who fostered his talent for engagement within the limits of architectural practice. Tom worked on numerous projects in conjunction with Olson and other partners as well as led his own projects in these journeyman years, and it is a testament to Olson and the culture of the firm that Tom was able to further his training as a professional without losing his individual voice. In 1994 Tom became a partner, along with Scott Allen, and the firm became Olson Sundberg Kundig Allen Architects.

A firm with four partners working collaboratively and individually has had many precedents in the past, with the influential postwar Italian firm BPPR and the Bay Area-based MLTW (Moore Lyndon Turnbull Whitaker) among the most famous. Olson Sundberg Kundig Allen Architects's collective work shares a commitment to the seamless union of art, design, and craft—a philosophy inherent in much of Northwest architecture—but the firm takes it to another level of interpretation and production that is all their own. This philosophy of engagement with the craftsmen and artists in the realm of architecture resonates profoundly with Tom's upbringing, and his commitment to it has further grounded these concerns for the firm. The commitment to materiality, craft, and construction manifests in

FIG. 4

FIG. 5

distinct ways for each of the partners. While Jim Olson's projects (especially his residences for art collectors) shows craft in an extremely refined manner of constructional connections and material finishes, Tom's work has tended to the other extreme. His designs often take on the simplest of spatial configuration, the most direct route of connections, the most straightforward of finishes; the refinement is found in the proportions and the details, but always in contrast to the larger, more elemental composition. In this way Tom's work is both representative of his firm and a departure from it.

THE HOUSES

The contrast and tension in Tom's work between inventiveness and refinement, elemental and exquisite, intuitive and super-crafted, can be found most clearly in his houses. Here, all the elements and working strategies that have defined Tom's mature work first came into being and continued to evolve and be refined from one house to the next, eventually leading to the larger commissions he now receives.

Craft

First and foremost, there is the idea of craft in each and every project. The commitment to the hand is second nature to his work, a legacy from his boyhood days with Balazs and his own collaborations with artists and craftsmen. Seattle and the Northwest have had long traditions of both wood- and metal-working, stemming from its lumber and industrial past. Tom brings this tradition forward in his work, beginning with the Studio House.

The Studio House (pp. 8–46) is unquestionably the watershed project in Tom's career. It takes all of his knowledge and experience from his early work and catapults it forward in a mature building. The project can be seen as a collaboration between Tom and the many craftsmen he brought to the project to produce a total work of art. The house was commissioned by Carol Bobo, a Seattle-based photographer who wanted a home that would double as a photo studio without losing the practicality or comfort of either. Although the site is suburban in nature, Tom came up with a scheme that was at once urbane and idyllic. A single glass, steel, and concrete volume houses the living spaces under a vaulted roof, allowing abundant light to come into the loftlike space while providing unimpeded views out to the lush landscape beyond. Adjustable screens and scrims modulate daylight as needed. While the tall trees of the surrounding landscape are echoed in the over-sized I-beams of the exterior steel frame, it is the smaller, human-scaled details within the space that hold the attention of the visitor. Tom has long been an ardent admirer of Pierre Chareau and Carlo Scarpa, whose works improbably bring the industrial nature of concrete and steel together with refined, jewelrylike detailings and finishes; the Studio House is very much in this lineage. Throughout the house, details large and small are exquisitely designed and realized in bronze, stainless steel, glass, and wood, among

FIG. 6   FIG. 7

other materials. These details punctuate larger expanses of concrete and rusting steel, often left raw to age natural-ly and gracefully. The most striking example of this combination of rawness and refinement can be seen in the kitchen island, a Chinese puzzle of crafted details (figures 6, 7; pp. 26–31). There are at least half a dozen separate parts, and as many crafts and craftsmen involved in its construction. The result is complex but not visually compli-cated. Each of the materials and their connections echo a larger part of the house and work in concert with it. The kitchen island—and the other elements such as the fireplace, the stairs, and the extensive built-in cabinetry—are akin to the custom furnishings in a Wright or Greene and Greene house: pieces of micro-architecture rather than dis-crete furniture. The traditions of the Arts and Crafts have often been disowned by the modernist movement, but here it is alive and well in the ultra-modern Studio House.

Clients

Although the Studio House can be seen as a quintessential example of a collaboration between craftsmen and the architect, it is also an ideal situation between architect and client. With the supportive feedback of Carol Bobo on many aspects of the house, the Studio House became full of wonderful and one-of-a-kind details. To a certain extent the same can be said for Jeff and Amy Larson at Chicken Point Cabin as well Michal Friedrich at the Delta Shelter. This is certainly true for The Brain Studio (pp. 54–76), which happens to be built across the street from the Studio House.

The clients of The Brain Studio, David Wild and Lulu Gargiulo, bought Carol Bobo's old house, and after seeing the Studio House commissioned Tom to build David a freestanding studio on their lot. David Wild is a video artist and director known for his offbeat short films and video work. Fitting a film director, David also has a strong, idiosyn-cratic visual style that manifests itself in his obsessions and collections: books, furniture, posters, and other cultural artifacts. Usually such an overwhelming personality can interfere with a strong architectural vision; in Tom's hands, however, David's quirks became the inspirations for the project. The seemingly straightforward box of the studio is actually slightly tapered on all sides, a design feature that also prevents noise reverberation. The experiential result is almost imperceptible yet still felt, and the analogy to David's personality—seemingly straightforward yet just slightly off—is undeniable. David himself admits that being in the studio is akin to "being inside my brain," and hence the name. At The Brain Studio Tom also utilized a strategy he called "the reinvention of the commodity" that informs so many signature moments of his subsequent work: an inserted loft in the studio is constructed from half-inch steel sheets, inspired by the material most often seen temporarily covering holes during road construction. Tom reinvented this mundane use by folding and welding the steel sheets into a sculptural, three-dimensional form, allowing the loft to be structurally self-sufficient. Commodity transformation, in this case from road work material to origami structure, is one of the hallmarks of Tom's work.

FIG. 8   FIG. 9

Gizmos

"The reinvention of the commodity" can take many different forms. In his next project, Chicken Point Cabin, Tom used a large steel pipe made for the Alaskan Oil Pipeline as a fireplace and converted an old steel coil into a table base. What Chicken Point Cabin became best known for, however, is the "Gizmo." Gizmos are what Tom calls the mechanical devices in his projects that turn static architectural elements into those with dynamic movement, often with the direct participation of the users. In a way the gizmos are also a reinvention or appropriation of engineering into the realm of architecture. Two of his most well-known gizmos are at the Chicken Point Cabin and the Delta Shelter, where hand-cranked mechanisms directly connect the architecture to its surrounding nature.

Chicken Point Cabin (pp. 78–108) was commissioned by Jeff and Amy Larson for their young family as a year-round weekend retreat. By coincidence, during an earlier visit to a nearby site in northern Idaho, Tom stumbled into a small cabin in the nearby woods that his family visited in the summer when he was growing up. Designed by Royal McClure, an architect contemporary of his father's generation, the cabin was a simple two-room structure stripped down to the barest architectural minimum (figure 8). Those summers at the McClure cabin, where "architecture" literally meant a room to get out of the occasional rain, made an incisive impact on Tom. When the Larsons asked for their cabin to directly engage its site, especially the spectacular lakefront views, Tom drew from his boyhood memories to design the Chicken Point Cabin. Working with the engineer/exhibit designer Phil Turner, Tom conceptualized a large, pivoting window wall of steel frame and glass infill that could literally open the lakeside facade of the house (figure 9). Utilizing a simple counter-balance principle where the two sides of the window's cross axel are nearly equal weight, the six-ton contraption can be open by hand-cranking the mechanical gears (pp. 94–97). The gizmo here, like the kitchen island at the Studio House, can seem overwrought in its verbal description but resolves into a visual and tactile delight. At the Delta Shelter (pp. 110–130) in eastern Washington, a similar device was designed to allow all four sides of the freestanding cabin on stilts to open simultaneously (pp. 124-125). Although the mechanical workings of the two gizmos differ in their details, the quest is the same: to open the architectural experience to a larger landscape.

Hot Rodding

These devices have garnered a lot of press for Tom and his work, and deservedly so, but most often it misses the point. While the gizmos' bravura combined with expert follow-through in execution make for great magazine and book fodder, Tom's true contribution is in how these experiments in new design stem from the desire to incorporate another vocabulary, another language of making into the rigid codes of today's architectural construction. The catch-all term that Tom uses to encompass his many conceptual and working techniques—from the reinvention of the

FIG. 10

FIG. 11

commodity to the gizmos—is *hot rodding*, itself a term borrowed from the customized car culture. Hot rod is traditionally the semi-underground movement where production cars are rebuilt using modified existing parts. In the hot rodding world the goal is to produce something completely unique not from purely raw parts (originally a condition of limited means and access) but from what pre-exists at hand. Since the original hot rodding of cars in 1960s southern California, the culture has seeped across to music (with sampling and the mash-up) and painting (postmodern collage) as well as film and television. Although there have been recent examples of hot rodding in architecture—the incorporation of old tankards or shipping containers by a few young firms—the intended result has been more rhetorical than as a working artifact. Additionally, these efforts are often presented as "prototypes" for large production runs, more in line with the current pre-fab obsession. Hot rodding, as it is reflected in Tom's work, is about the production of a unique, one-of-a-kind artifact. This manifests itself most clearly with the house that Tom and his wife Jeannie built for themselves appropriately named the Hot Rod House (pp. 134-171).

Tom and Jeannie bought a turn-of-the century house some years ago in an older Seattle neighborhood with the intention of someday hot rodding it. The two-story bungalow was stripped to its external walls, while foundation and floor plans were kept. The new house is woven within and on top of the pre-existing footprint, much like a custom hot rod car is often built on top of an old chassis. Initially, especially on the exterior, not much of the previous house can be detected. What is visible is seemingly all new construction: a steel I-beam structure framing large expanses of glass and wood shutters sit atop a new concrete perimeter wall. The entry sequence leads to a folded steel staircase that connects the three levels of the house. It is not until the middle floor, where the century-old wood floors are mostly kept while new enclosure walls are built around them, that the effects of an architectural hot rod are apparent (pp. 150-151). Tom methodically replaced walls where new load-bearing walls were required, and unsentimentally kept walls where replacements were not needed. The visual result is at once a surreal juxtaposition of old and new and relentlessly logical in its constructional economy. Tom cites budgetary constraints as the driving force for many of the more beautiful results of the house. The folded metal staircase that winds its way up the house (pp. 148-149), for example, triples in function as egress, lightwell, and built-in sculpture.

EXPERIMENTATION

Tom is not interested in creating a form that is repeatable ad infinitum; his ideas are constantly evolving. Experimentation and pushing materials and construction to their limits in one project allows the results to be refined in the next project. In the front steel-and-glass enclosure in the Hot Rod House Tom investigated a way of sealing the glass panes directly into the frame without any intermediate mullions or flashing, which visually bulks up the metal frame and distracts from the view. This literal stripping away of any mediated material allows the architecture to be

FIG. 12

FIG. 13

FIG. 14

its most elementary and basic. This strategy has shown up again in one of Tom's current projects, the Pratt Fine Arts Center for Seattle (figures 10, 11), where the raw, elemental language of material and connection first established in the Hot Rod House is translated into a large 40,000-square-foot public building.

Although the Pratt Fine Arts Center is not yet built, a similar translation from small experimental house to a larger construction is seen in the Mission Hill Family Estate Winery complex outside of Vancouver. Constructed mostly of concrete, Tom varied the experience of the many spaces through the subtle use of concrete construction. This is most clearly demonstrated in the main building (figure 12), where the underground walls and vaults of the majestic wine caves are constructed of pour-in-place concrete (figure 13), while the above-ground building and bell tower utilize pre-cast concrete panels (figure 14) that are craned into place. Tom parlayed his experience with concrete from the Studio House and the Brain Studio for the cast-in-place construction, while the pre-fab panels above-ground were gleaned from the Chapel of St. Ignatius at Seattle University by Steven Holl, Tom's old teacher who tapped Tom as the associate architect and collaborator on the project. The experience of a small studio and chapel cannot compare to a 200,000 square-foot multibuilding complex, but without the earlier experimentations it would have not been possible.

As Tom's architectural trajectory moves forward to larger public projects and recognition (he recently won the commission for the Sun Valley Center for Art in Idaho and was a finalist for the Cooper Hewitt's National Design Award in architecture), houses and the experimental opportunities they afford remains an essential part of his work. Tom continues to pursue residential work although they take as much time and pay a fraction of the fee that larger commissions bring. The experience of building the five houses included in this monograph and many others have proven to Tom that the small palette and often limited budget of a house can yield results far more satisfying and influential on his future work than the larger projects. Tom continues to view the house as the small seed that eventually yields the biggest of architectural fruit.

The clients of The Brain Studio asked Tom to design a free-standing addition to their home after seeing the Studio House. The result is dubbed "The Brain," and the primary occupant is David Wild, a film director. David wanted a studio where he could work on his personal projects—photography and writing.

David asked for as raw a space as possible, to be "finished" by the creative process that would happen inside it. The structure is a straightforward cast-in-place concrete box, punctured on two sides with large steel-case windows. Although it appears to be a true rectangular form, the studio's envelope is slightly tapered to prevent reverberation of sound, which happens with perfect right-angle corners and interferes with music listening.

The double-height single room of the main space is inserted with a loft constructed entirely of 1/2-inch steel plates that are welded and folded in an "origami" fashion in order to produce the rigidity and strength need to become structurally self-sufficient. A set of stairs to the loft is hidden behind a darkroom and storage space is tucked beneath the steel loft, while a fireman's pole provides an easier and more flamboyant means of egress down.

The Brain Studio is as much a treehouse, fort, and playroom as it is a serious work space, and ultimately it is a quirky but true reflection of the client and his personality. "Being in the studio is like being in my brain," David said to Tom at the beginning of the process, and the name for the project stuck.

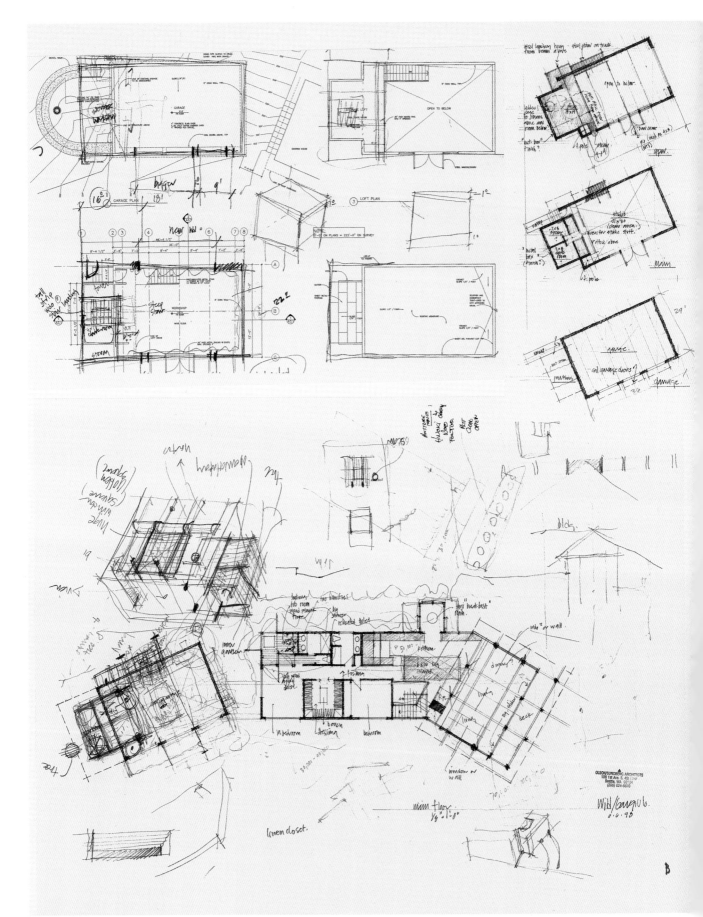

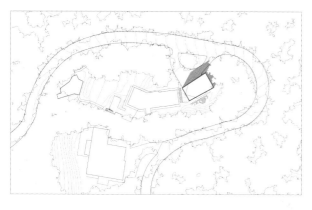

SITE PLAN

1 OPEN TO BELOW
2 WORK LOFT

LOFT LEVEL

1 STUDIO
2 DARKROOM
3 STORAGE

MAIN LEVEL

1 GARAGE
2 STORAGE

GARAGE LEVEL

0   5'   15'   35'

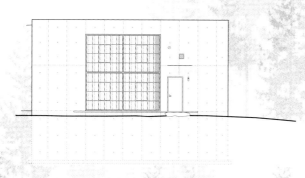

SOUTH ELEVATION

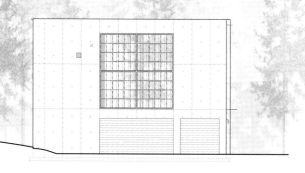

NORTH ELEVATION

EAST ELEVATION

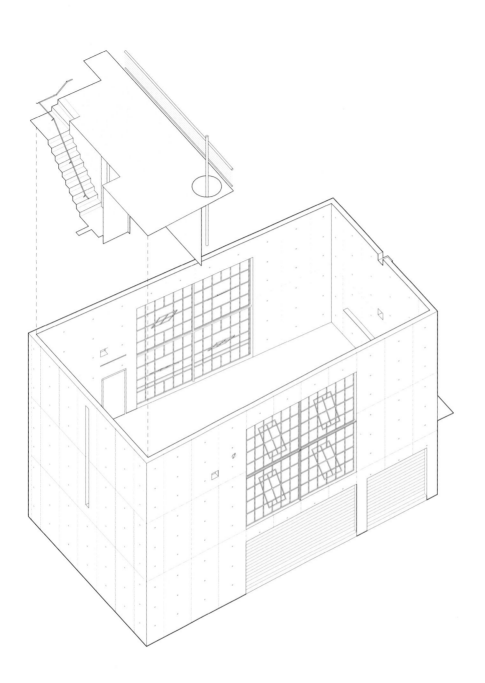

The entire loft structure, constructed entirely of 1/2-inch steel plates, is cast integrally into the concrete box. The material was inspired by road construction steel plates, which were then repurposed for another use in a process Tom calls the "reinvention of the commodity," the infusion of the poetics into the pragmatic and the mundane.

Floor-to-ceiling light-blocking curtains as well as theatrical scrims can be used to cover the large expanse of glass during film shoots and editing, while motorized industrial pulleys installed to lift heavy equipment are also used to hang the bare light bulbs.

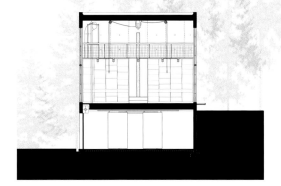

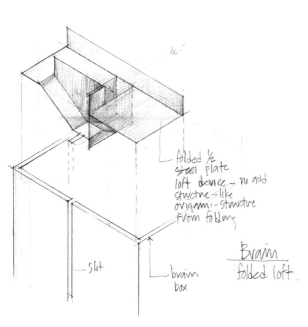

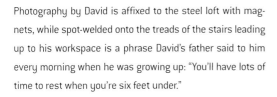

folded ½
steel plate
loft device — no add
structure —like
origami - structure
from folding

Brain
folded loft.

slot

brain
box

Photography by David is affixed to the steel loft with magnets, while spot-welded onto the treads of the stairs leading up to his workspace is a phrase David's father said to him every morning when he was growing up: "You'll have lots of time to rest when you're six feet under."

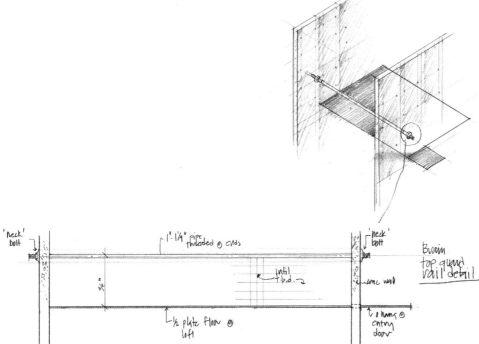

Brain
top guard
rail detail

'neck'
bolt

1"-1¼" pipe
threaded @ ends

'neck'
bolt

3½"

intl
t.b.d.

conc wall

½ plate floor @
loft

to hang @
entry
door

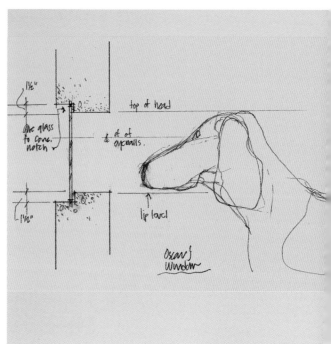

Oscar the hound dog, the other full-time occupant of the Brain, was given a special sentry window on the loft level for constant surveillance.

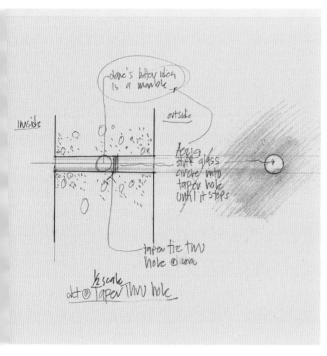

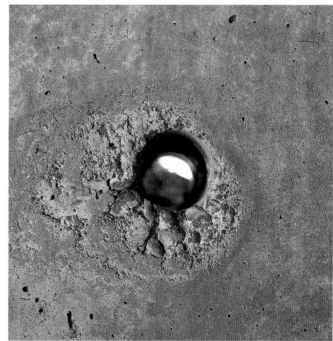

The holes left over from the concrete formwork were originally going to be plugged with glass disks, but David suggested the use of glass marbles instead. An inverted, *camera obscura* effect is seen through each oculus, appropriate for this film director and photographer.

I am looking at a photograph of the final studio review that I taught at the University of Washington in the spring of 1979. The subject, if I recall correctly, was a large urban hybrid building inserted into the city fabric of Seattle. Tom Kundig was one of my students (I think there were sixteen in all), and I remember he received the critical wrath of Rem Koolhaas with a puzzled silence. Rem had come all the way from Rotterdam and William Stout had flown in from San Francisco. Victor Steinbrueck was also a reviewer as were my inspirational professors Astra Zarina and Herman Pundt.

It is a pleasure to write this note on the brilliant built works of Tom Kundig as I frame my thoughts from this 1979 black-and-white photo. Twenty-seven years have passed since that warm spring day, and yet, if I think deeply it seems time has stopped. There are a handful of photos of different students getting up to defend their works in an atmosphere of serious excitement and fun. The frame brings together my initial education at the University of Washington, my roots in the Pacific Northwest, my great teachers, and the study year spent in Rome with Astra Zarina, as well as my year at the Architectural Association and the close friendship with Rem Koolhaas and William Stout, who carries on the torch at William Stout Books in San Francisco. These thoughts remind me that architecture is about spirit as much as thought and construction. Spirit and enthusiasm in a teacher equip a student not only with a principal teaching but also with the feeling that everything that is created has some effect, some impact, and that—especially in architecture—this zeal and dedication is transferred from teacher to student and from generation to generation. I remember the words of Louis Kahn, "There is no such thing as architecture, what exists is the spirit of architecture."

With the faith of every teacher is the possibility of quality within each student, and with the belief that we all have the possibility of being better, I urged Tom Kundig to stretch the theme of this book beyond houses, to urban issues and the social implications of public buildings. It is as if we are still in the basement classroom at the University of Washington!

Tom's larger contributions should also be acknowledged; his public works of architecture will bring inspired spaces with intense connections of material and detail to the joy of a greater number of individuals in the future. His positive mental thoughts, his core values, perhaps these are the conceptions of a "spirit of architecture" which is passed on and thrives in continuity and zeal.

CHICKEN POINT CABIN
HAYDEN LAKE, NORTHERN IDAHO
2000-2003

The owners of Chicken Point Cabin, Jeff and Amy Larson and their two young children, bought the waterfront property—located half an hour from their house in northern Idaho—in order to build a lakeside cabin. Their intent was to be able to use the house year-round, but especially during the summer, when the local weather can get oppressively hot. Their only directive to Tom was simple: make the house as open to the water as possible. Tom's response to this challenge was as direct as the request: a large pivoting picture window on the waterside that literally opens up to the landscape. "Little house, big window," in Tom's words.

This direct and powerful gesture imposed a multitude of design and technical challenges. At first a simple counter-balance device using sandbags was proposed, then a power-generated mechanical system that treats the twenty-foot-by-thirty-foot window as a large garage door. The desire to design something that required direct action by the user, however, proved to be too irresistible. The final solution is a hand-cranked mechanical contraption employing a counterbalance principle through a set of gears, like that of a bicycle, that allow minimal input of force to pivot the six-ton steel and glass window. Although the "Gizmo" (as Tom refers to it) employs sophisticated mechanical engineering, the result is not unlike the opening of a tent flap, allowing fresh air and unimpeded views to enter the cabin proper.

A plywood loft containing the master suite is suspended into the concrete-block shell and overlooks the living space, while additional bedrooms and service spaces are saddlebagged on the two sides of the main volume. Although the house is approached by water during the summer months by the family, during the winter the approach is from the road, and the house is entered through the nineteen-foot steel door on the west side. The Chicken Point Cabin was named after a natural landmark nearby, and since its construction has become a local sight in its own right.

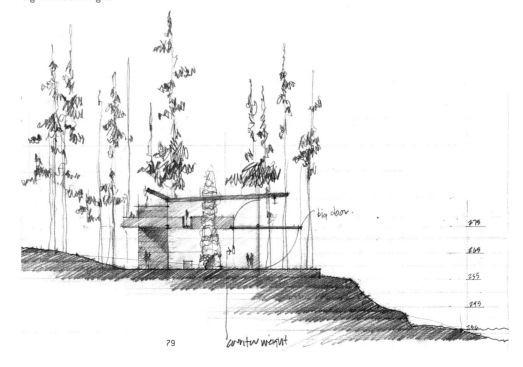

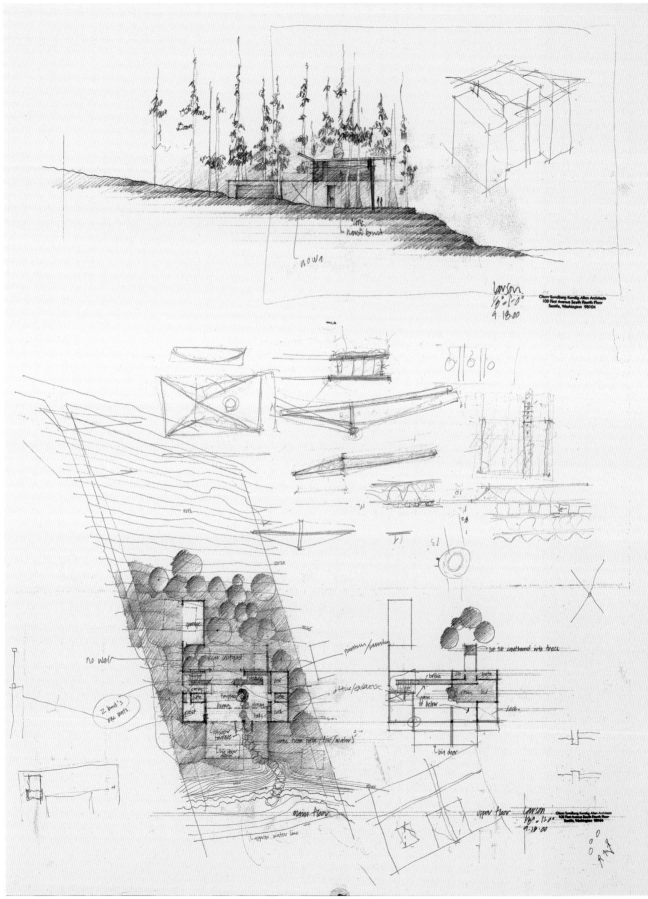

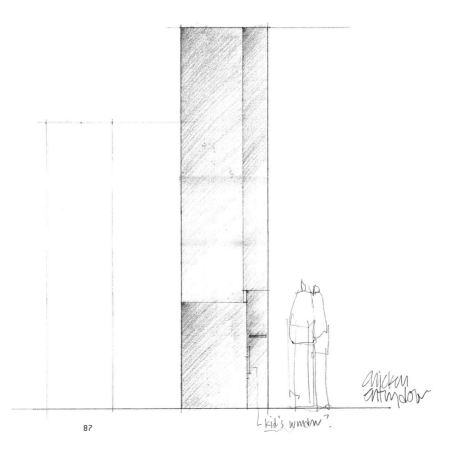

kid's window?

Although the house is relatively small and compact, the entry sequence is highly choreographed for dramatic effects. After passing through an imposing nineteen-foot metal door, which was scaled to the tall pines that surround the house, a tall set of stairs that leads to the second floor loft acts as sentry and screen of the kitchen and living room beyond. The hovering stairs is an extension of the plywood sleeping loft inserted into the double-height volume of the concrete-block frame.

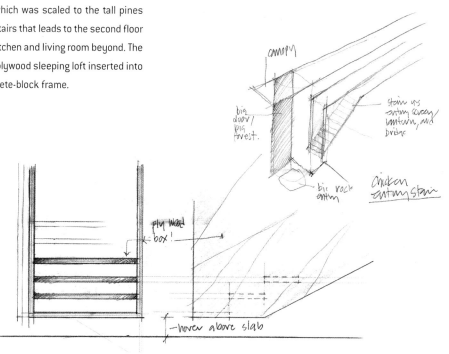

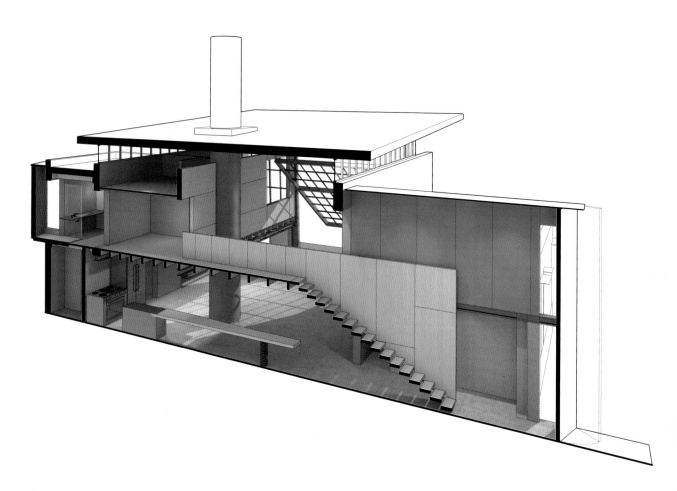

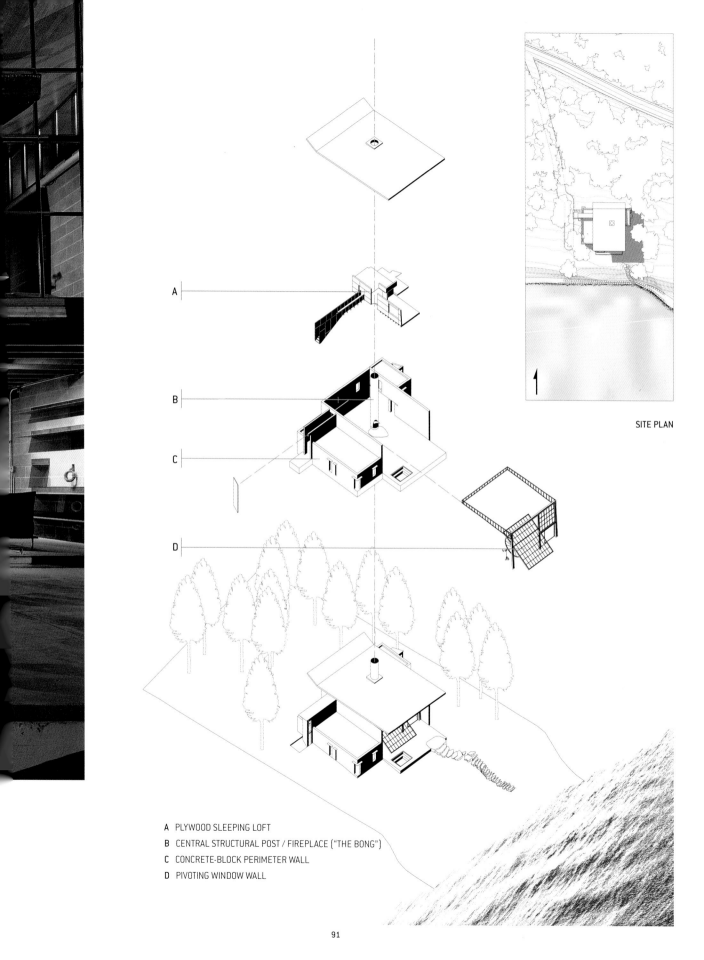

SITE PLAN

A PLYWOOD SLEEPING LOFT
B CENTRAL STRUCTURAL POST / FIREPLACE ("THE BONG")
C CONCRETE-BLOCK PERIMETER WALL
D PIVOTING WINDOW WALL

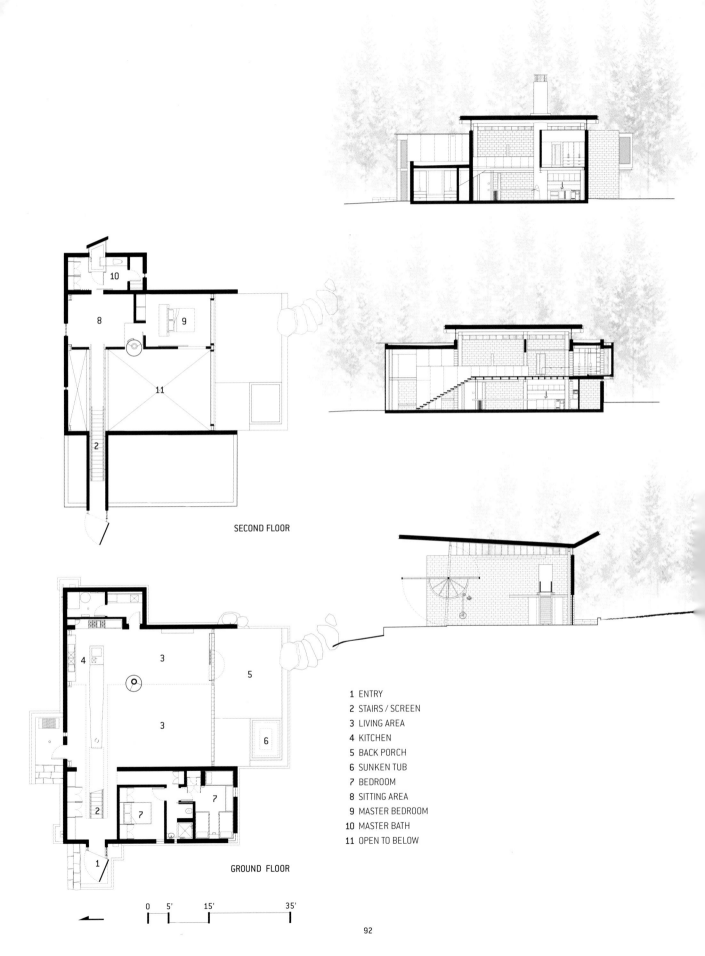

SECOND FLOOR

GROUND FLOOR

1 ENTRY
2 STAIRS / SCREEN
3 LIVING AREA
4 KITCHEN
5 BACK PORCH
6 SUNKEN TUB
7 BEDROOM
8 SITTING AREA
9 MASTER BEDROOM
10 MASTER BATH
11 OPEN TO BELOW

0   5'   15'   35'

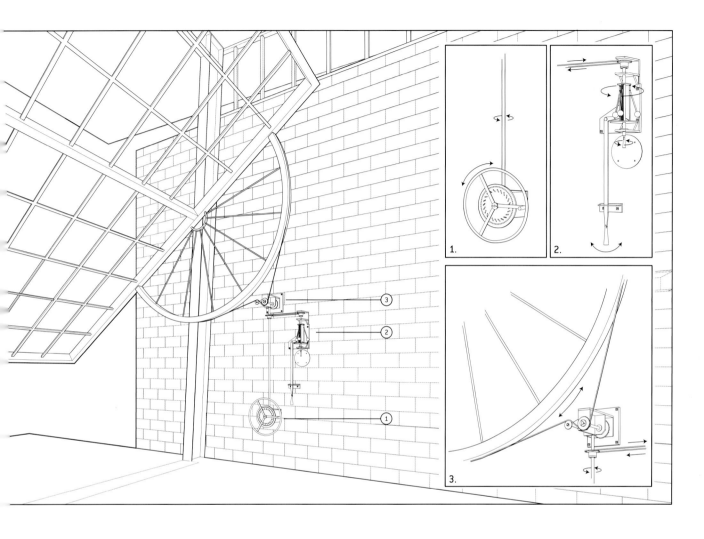

The Gizmo which opens and closes the large six-ton window, was conceptualized by Tom and engineered by Phil Turner, whose background in science exhibitions made him the ideal collaborator. Although the axel is located asymmetrically across the window in order to produce the overhead clearance needed when it is in the open position, the two halves, top and bottom, weigh about the same and are in equilibrium, therefore requiring very little exerted force to pivot it. A hand-operated wheel (1) turns the driveshaft (3) which in turn operates a set of gears fitted together, much like a bicycle in low gear, to produce the force to open the window. A flyball governor (2), a mechanical device that regulates and maintains the speed of the gears once they are in motion, was installed for safety. As the gears surpass a certain speed, the governor counteracts the additional speed by spinning in the opposite direction, and the pendulums swing out to sound a flat disk bell as a warning. Needless to say, the Gizmo was the favorite part of the house for six-year-old Clay Larson when it was built.

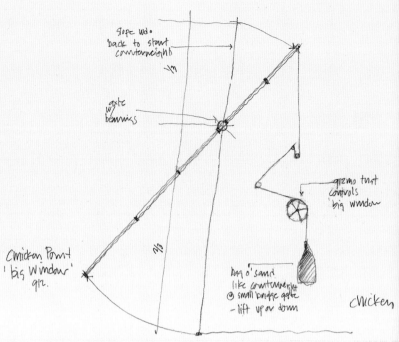

slope wo.
back to start
counterweight
1/4

gate
w/
bearings

slope wo.
gizmo that
controls
'big window'

Chicken Point
'big window'
gtz.

big o' sand
like counterweight
@ small bridge gate
- lift up or down

chicken

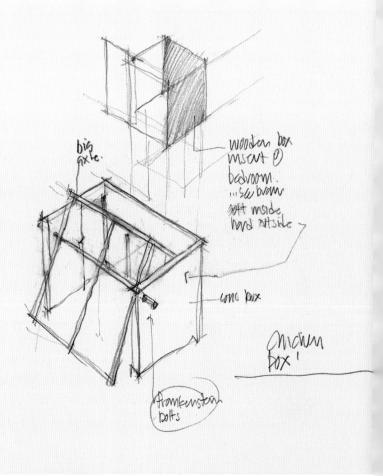

big
axle.

wooden box
insert @
bedroom.
...see brain
soft inside
hard outside

conc box

Chicken
box '

Frankenstein
bolts

The fireplace is constructed from a four-foot-diameter steel pipe left over from the Alaskan Oil Pipeline project. Acting as the proverbial hearth at the center of the house, it is also the structural post for the steel frame. The opening for the fireplace was notched at the angle, like the way a large Douglas fir would be harvested, and the leftover piece of steel becomes the fireplace hood. This piece was nicknamed "The Bong" because an early quarter-inch model of it resembled Washington state's newest legalized medical device.

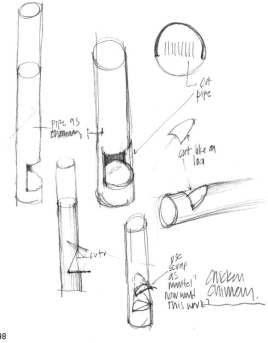

The kitchen island and dining table is set on axis with the front door, the stairs, and the bridge above. The table top is a single rough-edged slab of wood, supported by a recycled steel spring coil.

A bridge overlooks the living space from the second floor and leads to the master bedroom and bathroom. The fireplace pipe intersects the second-story plywood loft and doubles as a fireman's ladder to the kids' sleeping alcove above.

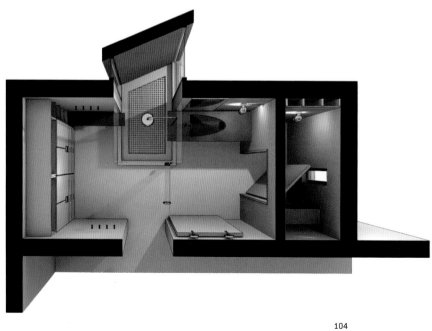

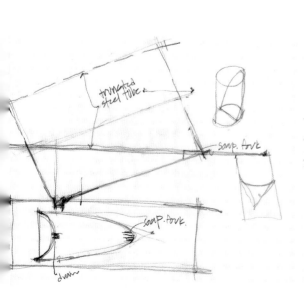

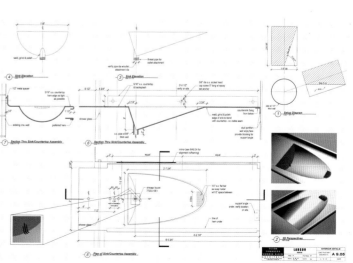

DOING

BILLIE TSIEN

If you spend time with small children they will teach you to look closely at things you take for granted, whether it is a special crack in the sidewalk or a feather found under a bush. This is a great gift. It gives the possibility of elevating the errand to ecstasy. As adults we spend so much time "accomplishing" tasks that we lose the ability to experience pleasure in the "doing."

The work of Tom Kundig takes your hand and says, "Stop for a moment and be aware of what you are doing and where you are." He accomplishes this by honoring simple activities.

He looks closely and makes things carefully. Whether opening a window or touching a stair railing—each time we are tugged, tapped, and whispered into paying attention. There is always an element of elegant invention. Our admiration for originality is balanced with our pleasure in "doing." He reminds us that small moments in life are precious. That is his gift to us.

The Delta Shelter was commissioned by Michal Friedrich as a weekend cabin for a site located on the flood banks of the Mazama River in eastern Washington. Because of seasonal flooding, the entire cabin was raised off the ground on stilts, which also heightened the 360-degree view of the natural setting. An added consideration was the need to close off the house in inclement weather when unused, while taking full advantage of the scenery when occupied.

Inspired by the pivoting window mechanism at the Chicken Point Cabin, Tom explored several options to open up the house, including shutters that swing open horizontally like large doors or vertically like propellers. In the end the most cost-effective solution was a set of four sliding double-height steel shutters that simultaneously open and close through hand-cranked mechanical means on the four sides of the house.

The remote location of the site also dictated that parts of the house had to be prefabricated off-site and trucked and assembled on site by mechanical fasteners. Only the interior finishes were done on-site. The Delta Shelter is clad in hot-rolled steel, which is left untreated and will rust and age naturally. The interior is equally raw, finished entirely in low-grade plywood and affordable cabinetry.

When in use, the Delta Shelter provides unparalleled views of the majestic landscape of rural Washington; when it is closed up, the cabin stands like a sentry among the aspen forest.

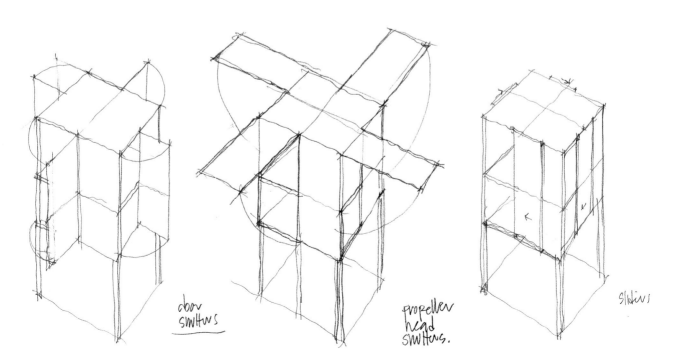

door
shutters

propeller
head
shutters.

sliders

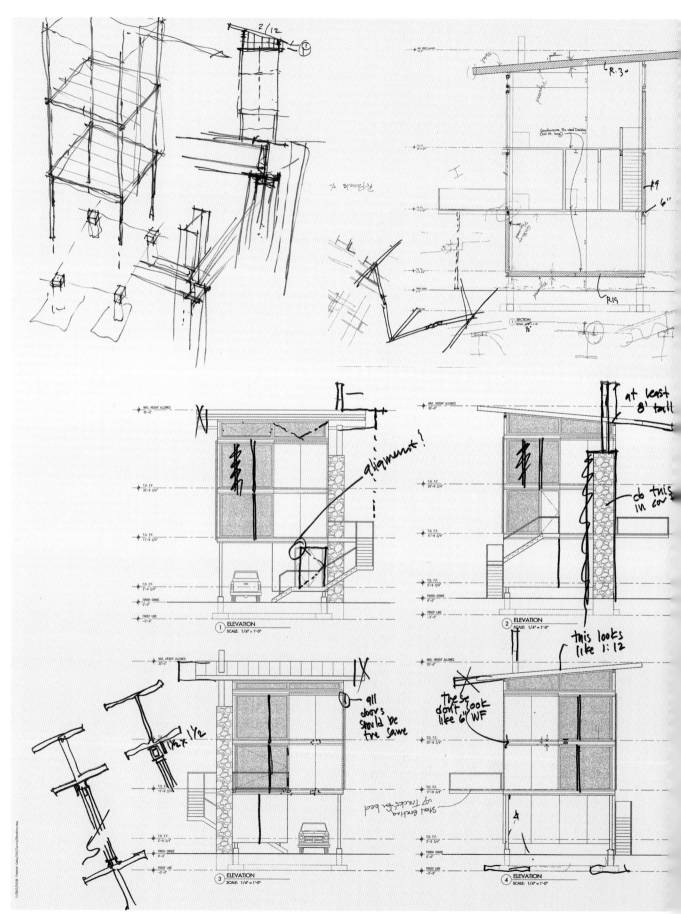

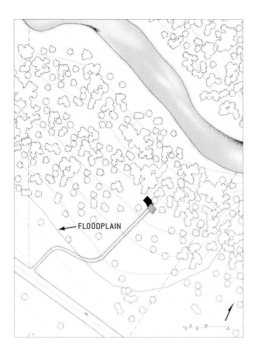

SITE PLAN

EAST ELEVATION

NORTH ELEVATION

SOUTH ELEVATION

WEST ELEVATION

1 LIVING AREA
2 DINING AREA
3 KITCHEN
4 BALCONY

LIVING LEVEL

1 ENTRY
2 BEDROOM
3 BATHROOM
4 BALCONY

SLEEPING LEVEL

1 STAIRS
2 STORAGE

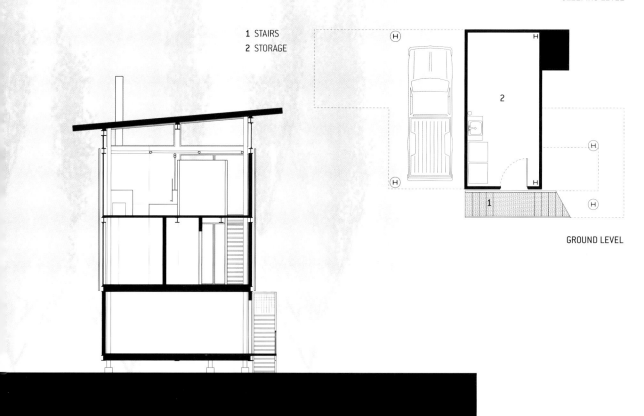

GROUND LEVEL

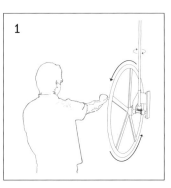

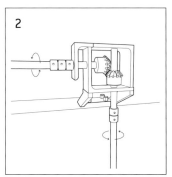

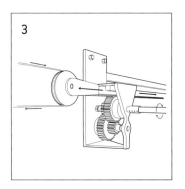

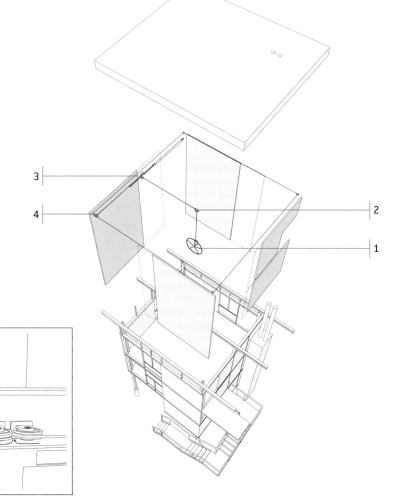

Collaborating with Phil Turner, who also engineered the large window gizmo at the Chicken Point Cabin, the mechanical device at the Delta Shelter presented a different set of challenges. Because the four rolling shutters are hung off the top of the cabin's structural frame, there is no counterbalance as a potential method to lighten the load. Consequently, the handwheel (1) transfers all the force in a direct manner through each of the bevel (2) and regular (3) gearshafts, except at the last connection where it becomes a 4-to-1 reduction shaft (4) to ease off the force on the pulleys. Unlike the system at Chicken Point Cabin, the mechanical system here at the Delta Shelter requires well-oiled parts and elbow grease to operate.

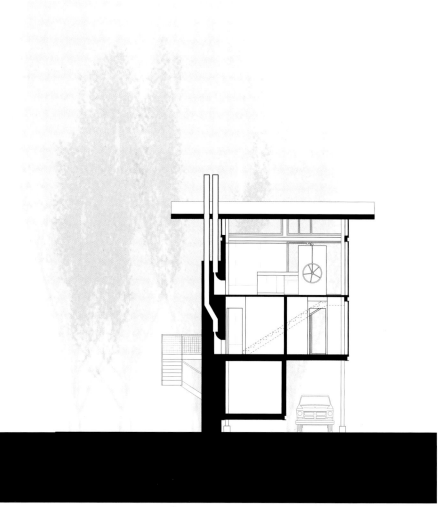

A DELICATE REFRAIN

RICK JOY

The etymology of the word *persona*, as derived from its Latin origins *personare* means "to sound through," and references ancient theatrical sources. Persona is synonymous with the projection of the "character," the resonant effect of the mask and the actor's voice "sounding through" intimately as it is projected outwardly to the audience. Analogously, the persona historically refers to the actual mask or more commonly the character via the role one assumes or precisely displays in various social, personal, and professional realms of real life.

As architects, we are challenged to reveal certain characteristics of ourselves, because for a few of us, our work exists on a mental plane that is personal for us and for our clients. For all however, we are also otherwise expected to respond fluidly to divergent external calls that are sometimes less personal than we wish. The static exists in the realm between our recognition of the outside world's perceptions, certainly as particular external expectations arise, and the developing persona that we choose to carefully put forth from within. I see this as positive, as one does not necessarily need to pretend or "sound through" a false personality, but contrarily, this invention allows one to simply express parts of one's real personality selectively as the situation demands.

The essential and distinct personas can be as diverse as the social milieus in which the architect is involved. With the client for example, the architect's roles range from very empathetic and loving to more of a teacher or guide. Similarly, the role of architect conforms to the situation: in engagements with other architects, on the construction site, as an academic, as a star when presenting his or her work to the public, or as a talent to be trusted when vying for an important commission. Respectively, the architect can also volunteer as a confidant, a moderator, a collaborator, a businessperson, or at times a performer, a director, a champion, an iconoclast, and, expectedly, a revolutionary. These various personas are then ideally less the emphasized presentation of a singular role and more the personification of the openness inherent in the profession. As the personality of the architect evolves, the challenge is to balance the extremes of the diverse milieus with one's own values.

While we expect a distinct personality in each architect, it is the openness and lightness in dealing with the demands on the persona that makes us genuine. Being present in the roles we are thrown into without loosing the overarching ideal of the persona can prevent us from disengaging from the real.

It is important to recognize, that within the projection of one's professional persona[s], there exists the potential that one may possibly identify too closely with the mask or role, most commonly the star role, and thus, somehow become disconnected from one's inner self. In the end, this all influences the architect's ability to achieve a level of human realness and personal generosity that is essential to the making of emotionally moving space.

I have known Tom Kundig, the maverick Seattle architect, for five years now. Through these years I have had a number of opportunities to visit him and tour his work. While his buildings are exemplary and highly spirited, it is his distinct personal presence in the work and in the lives of all involved that truly stands out for me. In each of the projects found on these pages, Tom reveals an empathetic sensitivity for his clients' desires, a deep understanding for the specificities of the settings, and the awareness of the architect's persona as a mediator between the corporeal and incorporeal realms of his design process. Instinctively following his strong convictions and personal interests, it's both his personality and his skillfulness in performing the personas of an architect that are evident throughout his work.

Perhaps the most obvious trait of Tom's work is displayed through his infatuations with what he terms "gizmos." Tom is an accomplished alpine climber often performing what he describes as "mixed treat climbs" on snow, ice, and rock cliffs. This world of ropes and carabiners certainly influences Tom's architectural details. Tom also described to me how he was a sculptor's assistant to Harold Balazs for some years in his youth. He attended the fabrication of large welded steel sculptures and developed a fascination for the makeshift machines and apparatuses used to move and balance the heavy pieces. Clearly the process of production became more irresistible than the actual finished works. This is reflected in his oeuvre, but even more so, Tom's work shows traces of how his interest in the planning and making of a house is a well-balanced process that doesn't end with its completion but is primarily an integrative part of its destiny. It takes a lot of courage to disclose and dedicate one's own fascinations so freshly.

Situated in a clearance on the edge of a lush flood plane, the Delta Shelter is an elevated scaffold-like house that enables one to rise high above the ground plane in search of views into the crowns of the surrounding trees. The ascension involves a sequence of compressed and extroverted spaces that is formalized in a windmill scheme of openings that rhythmically frame views from each of the four sides. This promenade architecturale extends out of the building and ends in the branches. With its stripped down aesthetics the house becomes an experiential device to explore the forest and the views.

The definition of a simple machine describes the ratio between the output force exerted on the load and the input force applied. The Delta Shelter makes the effort of ascending an entertaining experience, and the structure is felt as an alchemistic machine transforming the force of climbing into a light sensation. The same can be observed with the structure's relation to the natural setting where it appears either as a machine-made contrasting contaminant or a soft coexisting complement to the colors of the forest, while the effects change with the slow speed of the seasons.

Challenged to conceive a retreat on the shores of a lake in northern Idaho, Tom makes a statement with the Chicken Point Cabin, or rather he creates an architectural treatise on the longing and nostalgia inherent in such remote and picturesque places. The lake is large and the water extends to the distant mountains and around disappearing shore-lines. One is compelled to dream beyond the desire to set off to new shores, and rather coexist with the mental ground of this restlessness and the peacefulness of this setting. The place is polarized by the drama of simultane-ously arriving, leaving, and grounding oneself in the in-between. Tom created a theatrical stage for these sensitive moments. The steel portal, which is reminiscent of large-scale naval architecture, and the operable window, which is big enough to push a boat through, frame the domestic experience otherwise. In an archaic gesture, the fireplace gives the interior an identity and organizes it both spatially and structurally. Through the roughness of the materi-als, the proportions of the spaces, and especially the industrial size of the swinging window, the house has the vibe of a workshop, set up to house the production of the boat planned to sail off. In absence of the boat, the house is both a trace of and a platform for the latent desires arising at this place.

Evolved in the same spirit of reduced means similar to functional naval or industrial design, this house reads like a series of metaphors and citations. For example the fireplace recalls the chimneys of the early steamships and the Gizmo, as Tom refers to it, functions like a mechanism to operate a giant gangplank. Yet, it challenges our perception not only by the detection of these traceable traits, but rather comforts us in a general feeling of archetypal reassur-ance. The memories connoted are familiar, and they are meaningful in their emotional effect rather than through the referential precision of the setting in which they are positioned.

The Studio House is in essence a lifestyle proposal for loft style living yet set in a pastoral setting. Conceived for a photographer and her daughter, the spatial openness of the big room is a theatrical platform, offering varied and adaptable appropriations and settings. The flexible lighting, the changeable windows, the spatial mobility of the cur-tain and the modular furnishings support this idea.

Capturing our sympathies with an energetic exuberance that pulls us into the moment and makes us feel personally addressed, Tom reveals a unique approach and sensitivity for these clients. The house departs from the ordinary subtly through the vehicle of time. In a quite precise move of grounding the house on physical vestiges of a past construction, Tom ignites a sense of permanence in the house and presents the house with an inherited layer of history and personal memory.

The Studio House approaches the soft theme of memory also via architecturally framed atmospheric means as seen in the light qualities of the spaces and the almost storybook vignettes, such as the little wash rooms and creaking slab doors. I wonder what memories will forever remain with the young daughter.

The Brain Studio's function is to provide an instrument that can be played via the filmmaker's excursions into mental realms that foster his creativity. How far can architecture stimulate the inhabitant's mental ground while still preserving the spirit of the freeing openness that is crucial for creative dreaming? Creativity is as much dependent on the realm of absorption as it is on the release. And in the case of the Brain, these realms are purposefully composed to be all in one.

Written in a naturalistic rawness, it is assembled of real time elements and details such as the quite apparent mechanics of the lighting devices and comical moments like the insertion of the sliding pole. Young Tommy came out to play here. More witty than didactic, the performance draws amused attention to the dark—the elements are somehow not only old-fashioned in spirit, but also formal, functionalist mechanisms. Like an ideal prosthesis, the house supports the movements of its user—though this time they are through the depths of mind, digging into the realm of dreams and exploring creative release.

The program of the house reflects this duality with the steel insert, serving the library, workplace, and the adaptive space with the big openings. The former is dark, low, and compressed, reminiscent of a writer's private den with a dense air of stored information, while the latter is a flexible studio space that allows diverse activities with an openness provided by the glazing of the view outside into the forest. A flexible lighting system and heavy curtains support its adaptability. Both areas are distinguished in ambience but coexist within the same concrete container so that they can be experienced somewhat separately but not completely separately, thus blurring the completeness of either. With these changing intensities within the overall mood, inhabiting this space feels like comfortable clothing that is worn so well that it disappears, offering the mental extremes of being naked in one moment and warmly clothed in the next.

I believe Tom's success is grounded in the relaxedness and centeredness of one that devoutly performs a strong personal vocation, which allows him to master the personas that he chooses to present. Rejecting the self indulgent, Tom doesn't shy away from the profession's extremes of making a personal work and of dedicating his efforts to his clients. Maybe this is a key to who Tom is, and why I have such respect for him as a person, and which perhaps, is as important as what he creates. Yet with each of his projects he creates the spatial and emotional ease for very personal ways of inhabitation. This stimulating openness feels like the invitation to our very own interpretations, offering me to drift off and invent stories of my own.

With the descended Edison bulb fixtures in the main room of the Brain, I am reminded of the super star persona master Tom Cruise, in the opening scene of *Mission Impossible*, in character and balanced between his personal and professional personas. Having fallen to within an inch of the floor via his climbing rope gizmo, but he luckily stops short, remaining alive, suspended and poised in a delicate refrain.

The Hot Rod House was designed by Tom and Jeannie Kundig for themselves. Their original house was a turn–of–the–century bungalow purchased years ago for its views and affordable price in the then working class neighborhood of Queen Anne with the idea of eventually "hot rodding" it: to build a new house on top of the existing foundations and structural walls, leaving many parts of the original house intact, and in the process turning an old jalopy into the envy of the neighborhood.

In many instances, experiments in new or seldom–used construction methods that were safely tested in previous projects are pushed to the limits at the Hot Rod House. The prefab parts and assemble–on–site idea employed at the Delta Shelter, because of its remote location, were used here because of the difficult, steep site. Another instance is the stairs, a daring experiment in the folding and welding of steel plates to gain structural integrity. Although this was first tested with the loft at The Brain Studio, The Hot Rod stairs goes much further in size and scope, rising three stories and becoming a structural component of the new house. The biggest coup, however, was to get approval for the stairs from the city's building department, which was wary from the drawings that the stairs could even stand on its own.

In 2006 Tom and Jeannie moved into the rebuilt house; however, the house continues to be a living laboratory, with new additions made and old parts tinkered with periodically, as inspiration strikes and budget allows.

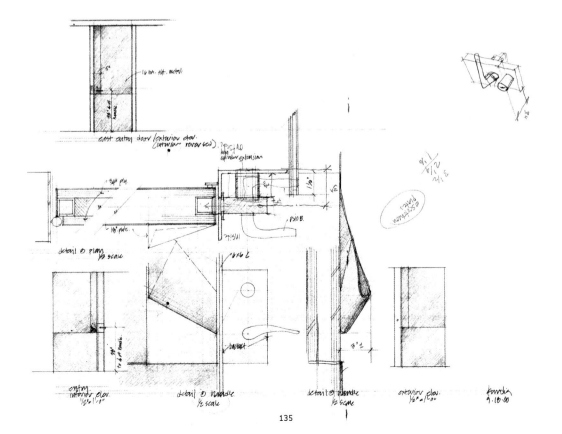

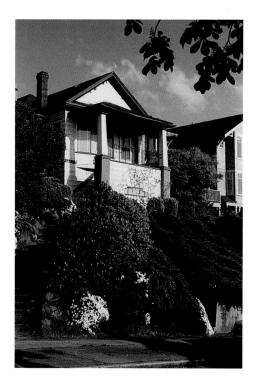

The house faces west toward the spectacular waters of Puget Sound and Elliott Bay. To maximize the view but also modulate the afternoon sun, the moment–frame structure of painted I–beams and glass becomes the framework for the sliding wood–slat shutters and infill panels. The asymmetrical placement of the new roof beam is due to the off–center location of the pre–existing structural line of the old house.

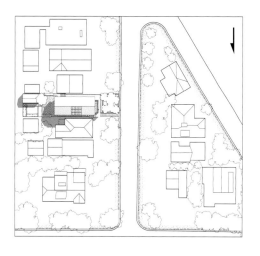

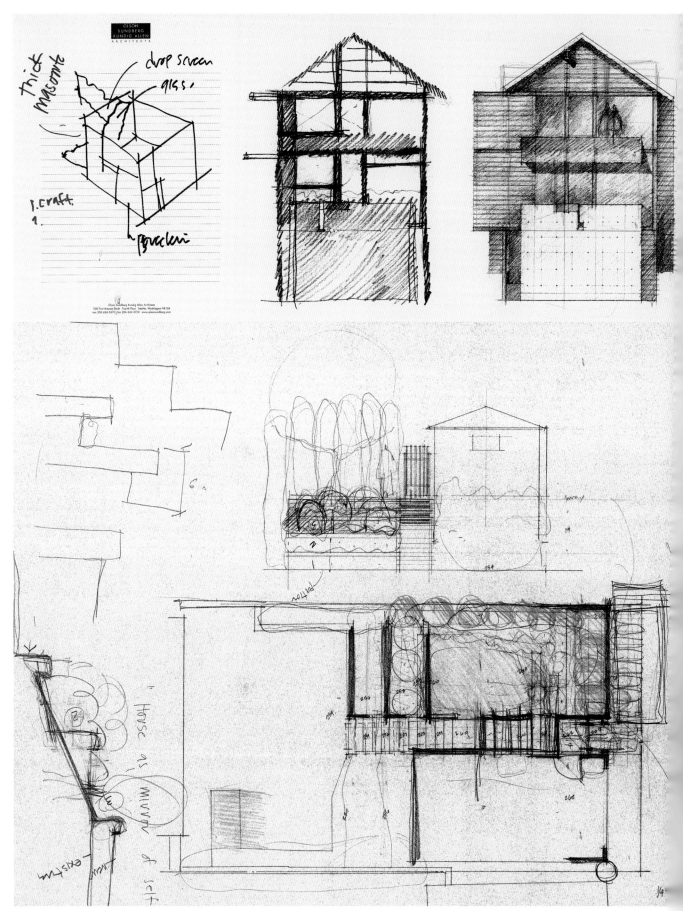

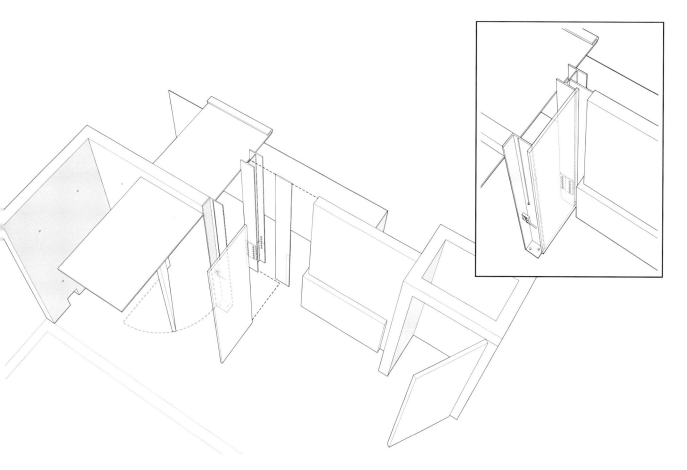

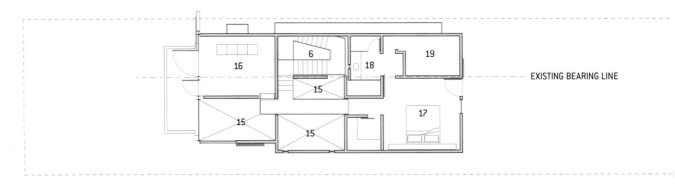

UPPER LEVEL

MAIN LEVEL

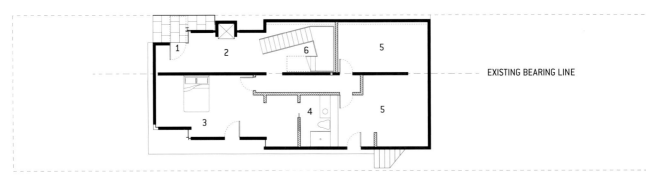

LOWER LEVEL

1 ENTRY
2 FOYER
3 GUEST ROOM
4 GUEST BATH
5 STORAGE
6 "THE DRAGON" STAIRCASE
7 DINING ROOM
8 LIVING ROOM
9 TERRACE
10 KITCHEN

11 PIANO ROOM
12 BACK GARDEN
13 GARAGE
14 BACK GATE
15 OPEN TO BELOW
16 "THE NEST" LOFT
17 MASTER BEDROOM
18 MASTER BATH
19 MASTER CLOSET

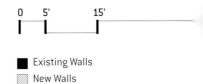

Existing Walls
New Walls

The house's original ground floor now houses the entry and guest bedroom, which is framed on two sides by the cast–in–place concrete perimeter wall. Tom and Jeannie lived here while the rest of the house was under construction, and the corner opening was dimensioned to Jeannie's chin at the bottom and the crown of Tom's head at the top.

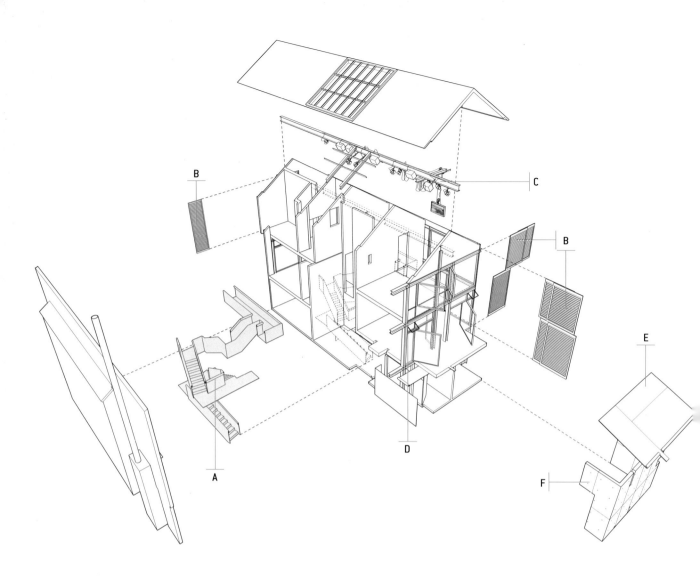

A Folded steel plate "Dragon" stairs
B Wood–slat sliding shutters
C I–beam armature for lights, speakers, and TV mover
D Structural moment frame / window wall
E Steel canopy
F Cast–in–place concrete perimeter wall

The new stairs—dubbed "The Dragon" by Tom because it twists and turns up the house like a Chinese dragon in flight—responds to the existing structure and the original layouts. The Dragon utilizes the principle of bending and folding sheet steel for structural strength, similar to the experiment first applied at The Brain Studio's loft. The Dragon exemplifies Tom's credo of "less doing more," so the stairs become egress, light well, structure, and art sculpture for the house.

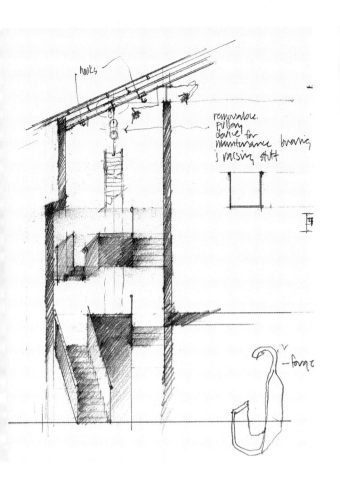

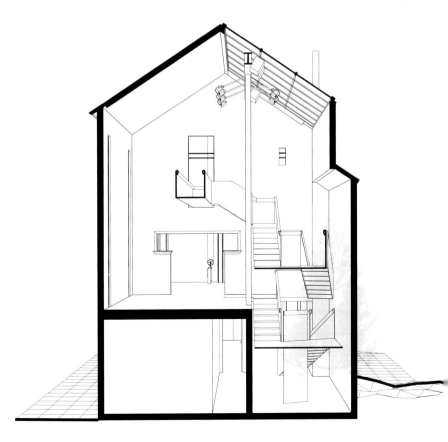

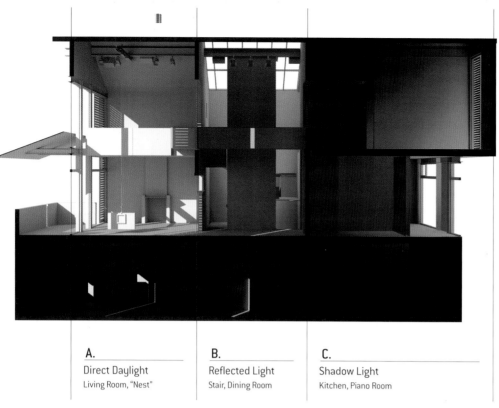

A.	**B.**	**C.**
Direct Daylight	Reflected Light	Shadow Light
Living Room, "Nest"	Stair, Dining Room	Kitchen, Piano Room

Much of the glass that affords the expansive view from the living room is set directly into the moment (structural steel) frame and sealed as minimally as possible. This deviates from the standard practice of intermediate mullions and requires customized hardware, but it does optimize the immediacy of the landscape beyond.

A TV mover device on pulleys drops a large TV screen normally resting in the "nest" above down into the living area as needed, seen in the photograph above framed by the old house's pre-existing room pass-through opening with its original molding. Tom worked with Phil Turner, who also engineered the gizmos at Chicken Point Cabin and the Delta Shelter.

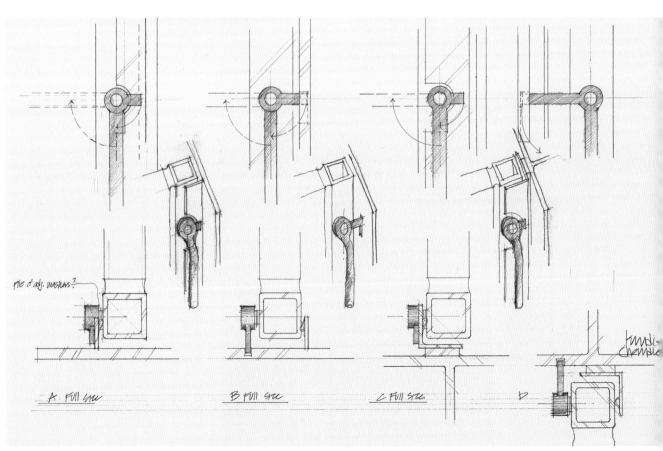

pile o' adj. washers?

A. FULL SIZE   B FULL SIZE   C FULL SIZE   D

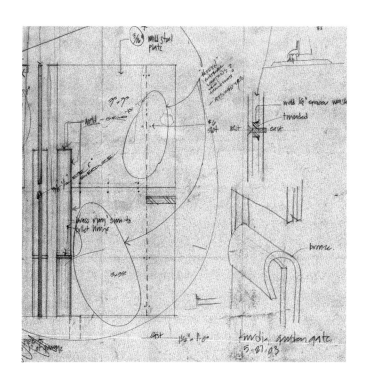

The back gate of the house, which leads to the back alley and garage, is simply constructed of leftover steel from the front entry and front canopy. Two layers of steel plates are sandwiched together with washer spacers in between and hung off a simple pipe over sleeve. A single strip of unpatinated bronze on the garden side is folded over the open slot to form the handle and provide a material contrast to the darkened steel.

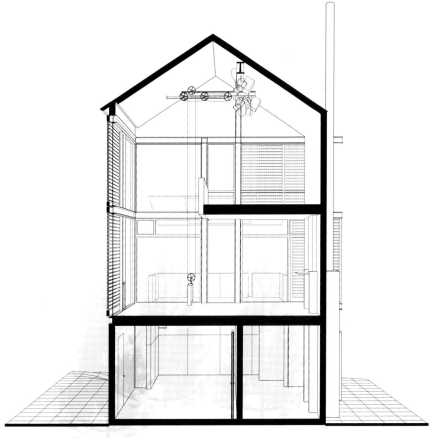

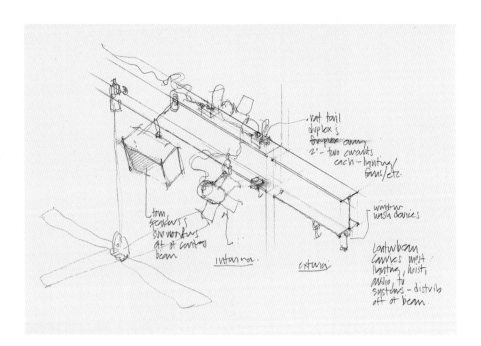

rat tail
duplex's
~~fireplace~~ ~~away~~
2' - two circuits
each - lighting/
fans/etc.

tom
speakers
suswinders
off of control
beam

<u>interior</u>

window
wash devices

<u>exterior</u>

Lantubeam
carries most
lighting, hoist,
audio, tv
systems - distrib
off at beam.

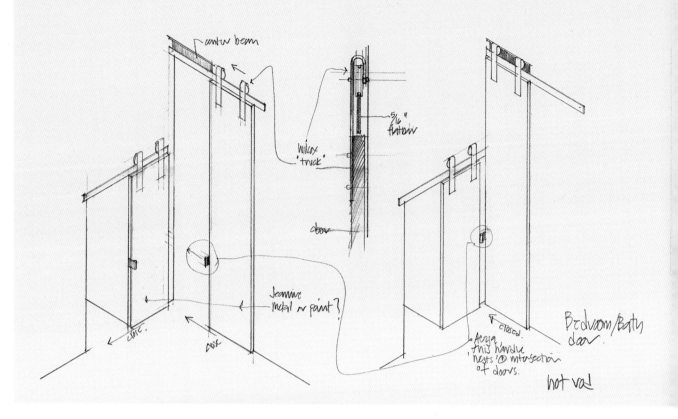

M. Heizer.

antur beam

5/16" flatau

wilox 'truck'

door

Jeanine
Metal or paint?

clos.

clos.

closed.

Bedroom/Bath
door.

Aerin,
this handle
nests @ intersection
of doors.

hot val

PROJECT CREDITS

STUDIO HOUSE
Client: Carol Bobo
Project Size: 7,200 square feet
Project Location: Seattle, Washington
Project Team: Tom Kundig, FAIA, design principal; Robert Jakubik, project manager; Aaron Schmidt
Consultants: Richard Haag Associates (landscape architecture); Janice Viekman (interior design contributor);
Monte Clark Engineering (structural engineering)
Craftspeople: Gulassa (uplights, fireplace, powder room sink, kitchen island, drop lights, master bathroom
cabinetry, cabinet finishes in kitchen, den, and guest room); Eisenwerk (gates, stairs, and entry drain runnel);
John Rizotto (powder room finishes, master bedroom cabinetry finishes); Dogpaw (kitchen island cast concrete counter
and doors); Empire Welding (structural steel); All New Glass (windows and big door)
Contractor: Charter Construction

THE BRAIN STUDIO
Client: David Wild & Lulu Gargiulo
Project Size: 1,000 square feet
Project Location: Seattle, Washington
Project Team: Tom Kundig, FAIA, design principal; Les Eerkes, Jim Graham, Joshua Brevoort
Consultants: Monte Clark Engineering (structural engineering)
Craftspeople: A&S windows (glass & steel windows); Aaron Schmidt (steel loft)
Contractor: d. Boone Construction

CHICKEN POINT CABIN
Client: Jeff & Amy Larson
Project Size: 3,400 square feet
Project Location: Northern Idaho
Project Team: Tom Kundig, FAIA, design principal; Steven Rainville, project manager; Debbie Kennedy,
interior design contributor
Consultants: Turner Exhibits (gizmo fabricator and engineer); Monte Clark Engineering (structural engineering); Moser, Inc.
(design/build mechanical system)
Craftspeople: All New Glass (big window); Star Steel (steel structure, bong fireplace); Steve Clark (table fabricator,
cabinets, beds)
Contractor: MC Construction

DELTA SHELTER
Client: Michal Friedrich
Project Size: 1,000 square feet
Project Location: Mazama, Washington
Project Team: Tom Kundig, FAIA, design principal; Ellen Cecil, project manager; Debbie Kennedy, interior design contributor
Consultants: Monte Clark Engineering (structural engineering); Turner Exhibits (shutter engineer and fabricator)
Craftspeople: Farwest Iron Works, Inc. (steel fabricators)
Contractor: Tim Tanner

HOT ROD HOUSE
Client: Tom & Jeannie Kundig
Project Size: 2,400 square feet
Project Location: Seattle, Washington
Project Team: Tom Kundig, FAIA, design principal; Jeannie Kundig, design contributor; Tom Kundig, staff architect
Consultants: Monte Clark (structural engineering); Rich Haag, Bruce Hinkley and Randy Allworth (landscape architects);
Turner Exhibits (TV mover engineer and fabricator); Cello Technologies (audio/technology/TV)
Craftspeople: Empire Welding (structural steel); Amick Metal Fabricators Inc. (custom metal bending, plate doors,
terrace roof, gates); Eisenwerk (specialty steel) Aaron Schmidt (stairs); Doug Wood (cabinets); Aesjza Munson (shutters);
Rhodes Architectural Stone (pavers)
Contractor: d. Boone Construction; with additional labor by Aesjza Munson and Tom Kundig-

EDUCATION

University of Washington, Masters of Architecture, 1981
University of Washington, Bachelor of Arts in Environmental Design, 1977, Magna Cum Laude
National AIA Scholar, 1981; Member: Phi Beta Kappa – Scholastic Honorary; Member: Tau Sigma Delta – Architectural Honorary

AWARDS

Architectural Record House, Delta Shelter, 2006
Residential Architect Grand Award, Delta Shelter, 2006
Fellow, The MacDowell Colony, Winter/Spring 2006
IIDA Northern Pacific Chapter INawards, Architects Office, 2005
Finalist – National Design Award for Architecture, The Smithsonian's Cooper–Hewitt National Design Museum, 2005
Residential Architect Grand Award, Chicken Point Cabin, 2005
Metropolitan Home Design 100, North Seattle Residence, 2005
AIA College of Fellows, 2004
AIA National Honor Award, Chicken Point Cabin, 2004
AIA National Honor Award, The Brain: a filmmaker's studio, 2004
The Chicago Athenaeum: Museum of Architecture and Design American Architecture Award, Chicken Point Cabin, 2004
Architectural League of New York, Emerging Architect: Tom Kundig, 2004
Masonry Institute of Washington Award, Lake House, 2004
AIA Northwest & Pacific Region Design Honor Award, Chicken Point Cabin, 2003
AIA Seattle Honor Award, Chicken Point Cabin, 2002
AIA Northwest & Pacific Region Design Honor Award, The Brain: a filmmaker's studio, 2001
AIA Seattle Honor Award, The Brain: a filmmaker's studio, 2000
AIA Summit 2000 Western International Design Merit Award, Studio House, 2000
AIA Seattle Conceptual Honor Award, The Brain: a filmmaker's studio, 1999
AIA National Honor Award (associate architect to Steven Holl), Chapel of St. Ignatius, 1999
AIA Northwest & Pacific Region Design Honor Award, Studio House, 1998
AIA National Design Award (associate architect to Steven Holl), Chapel of St. Ignatius, 1998
AIA Seattle Merit Award Studio House, 1997
AIA National Religious Architecture Award (associate architect to Steven Holl), Chapel of St. Ignatius, 1997
AIA Northwest & Pacific Region Design Honor Award, Urban Villa, 1997
AIA Seattle Citation Award, Urban Villa, 1996
AIA Seattle Conceptual Citation Award, Home House, 1996
AIA Northwest & Pacific Region Design Merit Award, The Meadow House, 1994
AIA Seattle Commendation Award, The Meadow House, 1993
Blueprint Award, Seattle Art Museum, 1981

EXHIBITED WORK

Seattle Architecture Foundation, "Ideas in Form 8," 2005; American Foundation for the Arts (New York, NY), "Restructure: New Forms in Architectural Mesh," 2005; National Building Museum, "Liquid Stone: New Architecture in Concrete," Mission Hill Winery, 2004; Washington State University, Department of Architecture, "Selected Work: 1997–Now," 2004; University of Washington, Department of Architecture, "Selected Work: 1997–Now," 2004; Architectural Institute of British Columbia (Vancouver, British Columbia), Wineries Exhibit, Mission Hill Winery, 2001; Kelowna Art Museum (Kelowna, British Columbia), "Mission Hill Winery," 2001; University of Washington, "Process House," 1998; Washington State University, "Tom Kundig: Work," 1998; Spokane Arts School, "Process House," 1997.

TEACHING/INSTRUCTION

Texas Tech University, College of Architecture, Visiting Design Critic, 2004; University of Oregon, Department of Landscape Architecture, Visiting Instructor in Kyoto, Japan, 2004; Harvard University GSD Seminar, Lecturer, 2003; University of Oregon, Visiting Design Critic in Kyoto, Japan, 2001; University of Washington, Department of Architecture, Lecturer, 1999; Washington State University, Department of Architecture, Visiting Design Critic, 1999; University of Washington, Graduate Design Studio, Instructor, 1999; University of Washington, Design Studio Critic, 1998–2001.

LECTURES

AIA National Convention, presenter, 2005; University of Washington, Dean's Lecture, 2005; Western Interiors & Design Conference (Los Angeles, CA), Panelist, Fall 2005; Cooper–Hewitt National Design Museum (New York, NY), Featured Speaker, Fall 2005; University of Washington, "New Wave of Structural Engineering in Architecture," Panelist, 2005; Sun Valley Center for the Arts (Ketchum, ID), Presenter, 2005; American Federation of the Arts (New York, NY), "Restructure: New Form in Architectural Mesh," Panelist, 2005; AIA Seattle, "Fellows Series: Tom Kundig FAIA", Lecturer, 2004; Architectural League of New York, "Emerging Architect," Featured Speaker, 2004; National Building Museum (Washington, D.C.), "Liquid Stone Exhibit," Guest Speaker, 2004; AIA Seattle, Panelist, 2004; AIA New York & Bulthaup Lecture Series, "Designing Around an Art Collection," Panelist, 2003; Art Basil/Miami Beach, "Architecture for Art: Collecting, Conserving and Exhibiting," Moderator, 2003; Western Interiors Design Conference (Cody, WY), Featured Speaker, 2003; PSU, Lecture, 2003; AIA New York City/Bulthaup Lecture Series, "Designing Around an Art Collection," Lecturer, 2003; AIA Northwest & Pacific Region Conference, Panelist, 2002; Architectural Institute of British Columbia, Winery Exhibit lecturer, 2001; University of Oregon Architectural Lecture Series, Featured Lecturer, 2000; Pilchuck Glass School, Lecturer, 1997; Spokane Art School, Lecturer, 1997; University of Washington, Department of Architecture, Visiting Design Critic, 1987–Present.

SELECTED BIBLIOGRAPHY

2006

Biel, Maria. "Life in Its Elemental Form." *BMW Magazine*, Jan. 2006, 32–36.

Kennedy, Lindsay. "Seattle 100: The People, Places and Things That Define Seattle Design." *Seattle Homes & Lifestyles*, Feb. 2006, 54–55.

Russell, James S. "In Washington State, Olson Sundberg Kundig Allen Sets Its Tiny Stilt Cabin Amid the Methow Valley's Four-season Splendor." *Architectural Record*, Apr. 2006, 92–97.

Viladas, Pilar. "Fortified." *New York Times Magazine*, Jan. 22, 2006, 63–69.

2005

Ballarín i Bargalló, Joaquim, ed. *Wood Houses*. New York: teNeues Publishing, 2005, 58–63.

Beard, Alison. "Erecting Altars to the Modernist Dream." *Financial Times*, Oct. 22–23, 2005.

Bossick, Karen. "Seattle Architect Chosen to Design Sun Valley Arts Center." *Hailey (ID) Wood River Journal*, July 6, 2005.

Broto, Carles. *Compact Houses*. Links International, 2005, 48–57.

Burnham, Michael. "Romancing the Stone: Concrete Claims New Sex Appeal." *Sustainable Industries*, Apr. 2005, 18–21.

Cañizares, Ana G. *150 Best House Ideas*. New York: Collins Design, 2005, 388–95.

Capullo, Lori. "Balancing Act." *Modernista*, Spring–Summer 2005, 36–40.

Drueding, Meghan, et al. "Residential Architect Design Awards 2005." *Residential Architect*, May 2005, 44–45.

Enlow, Clair. "Flexible Walls Let Gallery Owners Move the Art." *Seattle Daily Journal of Commerce*, Oct. 5, 2005.

———. "Thinking Inside the Box." *Seattle Times Pacific Northwest Magazine*, May 22, 2005, 12–19.

Gragg, Randy. "Portland Has Design Expertise; It Must Learn to Export It." *Portland Oregonian*, July 17, 2005.

Igoe, Kelly. "Seattle National Design Award Finalists." *Arcade* (Northwest Architectural League), Autumn 2005, 11.

Interior Design. Newsdesk. July 2005.

Janjigian, Robert. "Awards Honor Style Innovators." *Palm Beach Daily News*, June 26, 2005.

Larsen, Jeff. "High-end Resort Rises High Above the Gorge." *Seattle Post-Intelligencer*, July 21, 2005.

Lubell, Sam. "Five Cubes and a Blimp." *Architectural Record*, Apr. 2005, 120.

Lutyens, Dominic. "Their Own Private Idaho." *Elle Decoration*, UK Edition, Aug. 2005, 88–97.

Marx, Thea. *Contemporary Western Design*. Layton, UT: Gibbs Smith Publishing, 2005, 28–29.

McCormick, Kathy. "Concrete Solution: House First in Calgary for Seattle Designer." *Calgary (Alberta) Herald*, Oct. 24, 2005.

"Open House." *Trends* 21, no. 17, (2005): 80–87.

Parks, Mackenzie Dawson. "Gray Matter." *City*, Spring 2005, 56–61.

Seattle Daily Journal of Commerce, "Kundig Finalist for Cooper-Hewitt Award." June 22, 2005.

Stadler, Matthew. "Steeling Beauty." *Metropolitan Home*, May 2005, 142–49.

Sun Valley Idaho Mountain Express, "Architect Chosen for SVCA," July 6, 2005.

Talarico, Wendy, ed. *Graphic Standards Details: Openings*. Hoboken, NJ: Wiley, 2005, 1, 20–27.

Viladas, Pilar. *Domesticities: At Home with The New York Times Magazine*, New York: Bulfinch Press, 2005, 150–56.

Webb, Michael. *Adventurous Wine Architecture*. Mulgrave, VIC (Aus.): Images Publishing Group, 2005, 134–41.

———. *Art Invention House*. New York: Rizzoli, 2005, 244–51.

Western Interiors & Design. "Seattle Space Odyssey." Mar.–Apr. 2005, 30.

2004

50 of the World's Best Apartments. Mulgrave, VIC (Aus.): Images Publishing Group, 2004, 124–31, 156–63.

Architects Newspaper, "Hearing Voices," Mar. 9, 2004.

Architectural Record. "AIA Honor Awards 2004." June 2004, 141, 143.

Bermejo, Rafael Fernandez. "Casa Chicken Point Cabin, Idaho." *Diseno Interior*, Oct. 2004, 130–37.

Bernstein, Fred A. *Metropolitan Home: Renovate*. Filipacchi Publishing, 2004, 156–61.

Casamonti, Marco, and Vincenzo Pavan. *Cantine: Architetture 1990–2005*. Federico Motta Editore, 2004, 186–93.

Céspedes, Analya. "Abierta Al Lago." *Vivienda Decoración*, Mar. 20, 2004, 32.

Cygelman, Adele. "Best of the Best 2004." *Robb Report*, June 2004, 272–73.

Daily Journal of Commerce, "NW Architects Win 4 National Awards," Jan. 12, 2004.

Dana, Karine. "Agence de Publicité." *AMC Le Moniteur Architecture*, Dec. 2004, 101–3.

Departures. "Merging Divergent Styles." May–June 2004, 183.

Enlow, Clair. "Machine Language." *Metropolis*, July 2004, 54.

Meill, Augusta. "The Offices of Olson Sundberg Kundig Allen Architects." *Workspace* 1, no.1, 44–45.

Ojeda, Oscar Riera, and James McCown. *Architecture in Detail: Colors*. Gloucester, Mass.: Rockport Publishers, 2004, 128–29.

"Open House." *Trends* 20, no. 8, (2004): 32–41.

Paul, Linda Leigh. *The Cabin Book*. New York: Universe Publishing, 2004, 150–59.

"Picture This." *Trends* 20, no. 1, (2004): 6–13.

Prinsen, Pauline. "Mission Hill Family Estate." *Objekt* (Neth.), no. 27, (2004): 90–91.

Rhodes, Elizabeth. "Seattle's Kundig Wins 2 AIA Awards." *Seattle Times*, Jan. 18, 2004.

Richards, Peter. *Wineries with Style*. London: Mitchell Beazley, 2004, 111–14.

Seattle Magazine. "The Power 25: The Building Blocks." Nov. 2004, 76–77.

Shapiro, Amelia. "Mission Hill Time." *Wine Country Living*, June 2004, 48–55.

Trulove, James Grayson. *Cottages: The New Style*. New York: Harper Design International, 2004, 122–39.

Viladas, Pilar. "Ferien im flugzeugangar." *Häuser*, Mar. 2004, 78–84.

Webb, Michael. "An Open and Shut Case." *Frame* (Neth.), Nov.–Dec. 2004, 102–9.

———. "The Spectacular Vernacular." *Frame* (Neth.), July–Aug. 2004, 102–9.

Weber, Cheryl. "Northern Lights." *Residential Architect*, Sept.–Oct. 2004, 76–87.

2003

Beaver, Robyn. *Another 100 of the World's Best Houses*. Mulgrave, VIC (Aus.): Images Publishing Group, 2003, 246–49.

Carrington, Dora. "Cubo magico con vista lago." *D Casa*, Sept. 6, 2003, 86–95.

Fonk, Hans. "Seattle All Stars." *Objekt* (Neth.), no. 24, (2001): 178–89.

Glass. "Pratt Seattle Plan Major Addition." No. 92, (Fall 2003): 14.

Gregutt, Paul. "Oh, Canada." *Seattle Times Pacific Northwest Magazine*, June 29, 2003, 12.

———. "Northwest Living: Everything in Place." *Seattle Times Pacific Northwest Magazine*, Nov. 2, 2003, 38–40.

Guzowski, Mary. *Daylighting for Sustainable Design*. New York: McGraw-Hill, 2000, 67–68, 70–73.

Hira, Savitha. "Steel Apartment." *Home Review* 2, no. 4, (2003): 53–60.

Meill, Augusta. "Practicing Out There, the View from Harvard." *OfficeInsight*, July 21, 2003.

Ngo, Dung. *World House Now*. New York: Universe Publishing, 2003, 184–91.

Ojeda, Oscar Riera, and Mark Pasnik. *Architecture in Detail: Materials*. Gloucester, Mass.: Rockport Publishers, 2003, 58–63, 130–31.

———. *Architecture in Detail: Elements*. Gloucester, Mass.: Rockport Publishers, 2003, 108–9, 114–15.

Olson, Sheri. "Into the Woods." *Western Interiors and Design*. May–June 2003, 44–53.

———. "Adaptive Reuse, Beyond Bricolage." *Architectural Record*, July 2003, 150–52.

Pearson, Clifford. "Wineries: Premier Cru Design." *Architectural Record*, May 2003, 241, 248–51.

Renzi, Jen. "Back On Line." *Interior Design*, May 2003, 290–97.

Shearer, David. "Nonconformists." *Clear* 3, no. 4, (2003): 40.

Trulove, James Grayson, and Il Kim. *The New American House 4*. New York: Whitney Library of Design, 2003, 142–55, 214–23.

Viladas, Pilar. "Open House." *New York Times*, Home Design, Part 2, Spring 2003, 64–74.

Woo, Youngmin. "Ridge House, Washington." *Haute*, July 2003, 97–102.

2002

San Pietro, Silvia, and Paolo Gallo. *Bagni*. Milan: Edizioni L'Archivolto, 2002, 60–61.

Trulove, James Grayson. *Private Towers*. New York: Harper Collins, 2002, 88–105.

———. *The Smart House*. New York: Harper Collins, 2002, 56–71.

———. *25 Houses Under 2,500 Square Feet*. New York: Harper Collins, 2002, 70–79.

Viladas, Pilar. "Think Tank." *New York Times Magazine*, Apr. 28, 2002, 88–89.

Webb, Michael. *Beach Houses*. New York: Harper Collins, 2002, 110–15.

2001

Gill, Alexandra. "Napa North." *Toronto Globe and Mail*, Oct. 20, 2001.

Henderson, Justin. *Design Secrets: Architectural Interiors*. Gloucester, Mass.: Rockport Publishers, 2001, 6–13.

Iovine, Julie. "Muscle Houses Trying to Live Lean." *New York Times*, Aug. 30, 2001.

International Architecture Yearbook No. 7. Mulgrave, VIC (Aus.): Images Publishing Group, 196.

MacQueen, Ken. "Mike's Little Secret." *MacLean's* (Ca.), Aug. 27, 2001, 36–37.

Trulove, James Grayson, and Il Kim, eds. *The New American House 3: Innovations in Residential Design and Construction: 30 Case Studies*. New York: Whitney Library of Design, 2001, 6, 94–103, 244–51.

Van der Neut, Ruud. "Olson Sundberg Kundig Allen," *Objekt* (Neth.), no. 18, 2001, 114–25.

Vercelloni, Matteo, et al. *New American Houses 2: Country, Sea & Cities*. Milan: Edizioni L'Archivolto, 2001, 108–32.

2000

Albert, Fred. "In der Sonne des Pazific." *Häuser*, Jan. 2000, 26–34.

Book, Jeff. "Scene Steeler." *Metropolitan Home*, Sept.–Oct. 2000, 184–89.

Cohen, Edie. "Seamless in Seattle." *Interior Design*, Mar. 2000, 202–7.

———. *West Coast Rooms*. Gloucester, Mass.: Rockport Publishers, 2000, 112–15.

Ojeda, Oscar Riera, ed. *The Best of American Houses*. Madrid: Kliczkowski Publisher, 2000, 128–43.

Toy, Maggie. *Practically Minimal*. London: Thames and Hudson, 2000, 72–73.

Vercelloni, Matteo. "A Seattle: Studio House." *InterniAnnual Casa 2000*, no. 3, (2000): 30–35.

Wellwood, John. "Mission Accomplished." *Western Living*, Sept. 2000, 46–50, 75.

1999

Medgyesi, Victoria. "Minimal, Elemental." *Seattle Times Pacific Northwest Magazine*, Oct. 24, 1999, 40–46.

Olson, Sheri. "Among the Houseboats." *Seattle Times Pacific Northwest Magazine*, May 23, 1999, 12–13, 22–24.

Viladas, Pilar. "The Iconoclast." *New York Times Magazine*, Oct. 3, 1999, 71–77.

1998

Cole, Katherine. "Laws of Nature." *Chicago Social*, Sept. 1998, 164–69.

Henderson, Justin. "Heavy Metals." *Seattle Magazine*, Jan. 1998, 36–40.

McMillian, Elizabeth, ed. *Living on the Water*. London: Thames and Hudson, 1998, 88–93.

Ojeda, Oscar Riera, ed. *Olson Sundberg Architects: Casas Internacional #59*. Madrid: Kliczkowski Publisher, 1998.

1997

Niles, Bo, ed. *Timeless Design*. Glen Cove, NY: PBC International, 1997, 58–59.

Ojeda, Oscar Riera, ed. *The New American House 2: Innovations in Residential Design and Construction: 30 Case Studies*. New York: Whitney Library of Design, 1997, 20–27.

Timmons, Deirdre Allen. "A View from the Top." *Seattle Homes & Lifestyles*, Apr. 1997, 42–47.

1996

Henderson, Justin. "Olson Sundberg with Terry Hunziker." *Interior Design*, May, 1996, 220–25.

Iovine, Julie V. "Essences of Ease." *New York Times Magazine*, Apr. 14, 1996, 19.

1995

Henderson, Justin. "Hauberg House." *Interiors*, Apr. 1995, 66–71.

Whiteley, Peter O. "A Box Seat on Puget Sound." *Sunset Magazine*, Oct. 1995, 98.

Whiteson, Leon. "A Balance with Nature on Puget Sound." *Architectural Digest*, Apr. 1995, 126–33.

1994

Canty, Donald. "Earth Cycle." *Progressive Architecture*, June 1994, 84–91.

Russell, James S. "Meadow House, King County, Washington." *Architectural Record*, Apr. 1994, 33.

Viladas, Pilar. "Sleekness in Seattle." *Architectural Digest*, Aug. 1994, 130–36.

1993

Albert, Fred. "House of Glass." *Seattle Magazine*, Apr. 1993, 40–43.

———. "Site and Sound." *Seattle Times Pacific Northwest Magazine*, May 9, 1993, 34–38.

Henderson, Justin. "Getting Away At Home." *Alaska*, Aug. 1993, 27–29, 39, 41.

Louie, Elaine. "People Who Live in a Glass House Love All the Light." *New York Times*, Mar. 18, 1993.

1992

Novitski, B. J. "Controlling Direct Sunlight." *Architecture*, June 1992, 113.

1990

Canty, Donald J. "Jewel Box." *Architectural Record*, Aug. 1990, 14.

PHOTO CREDITS

Published by
Princeton Architectural Press
202 Warren Street
Hudson, New York 12534
www.papress.com

Editor: Jennifer N. Thompson
Design: Dung Ngo

ISBN 978-1-64896-054-3

The Library of Congress has cataloged the hardcover edition of this book as:
Tom Kundig : houses / Dung Ngo, editor ; with contributions by Steven
Holl, Rick Joy, Billie Tsien.
176 p. : ill. (chiefly col.) ; 26 cm.
Includes bibliographical references.
ISBN-13: 978-1-56898-605-0 (hardcover : alk. paper)
1. Kundig, Tom—Criticism and interpretation. 2. Architect–
designed houses—United States. 3. Architecture—United States—21st
century. I. Ngo, Dung. II. Kundig, Tom.
NA737.K86T66 2006
728.092—dc22 2006017979